CU00693793

Homecoming 2

Winter Solstice 2023

KIN

Aurochs Underground Press

Homecoming

Aurochs 2: Homecoming

ISBN 978-1-7396972-4-2

Published by Aurochs Underground Press, Bath, UK

HOMECOMING

A Journal of New Animist Writing

Edited by Jack Wolf

Homecoming

List of Artworks:

Homecoming

Contents:

Homecoming

Kinship: Personal and Universal
Philip Shallcrass

For most of human history, animism was the foundation on which all our relationships with the world were based. It flourished especially amongst humans whose ways of life relied on foraging for plants and hunting other animal persons for food, clothing, shelter and the manufacture of tools, musical instruments, toys, weapons and other artefacts. This hunter-gatherer lifestyle spanned much of human history and all of prehistory. In post-industrial societies, the only contact most of us have with living animals is keeping a pet. We buy prepared meat in sealed wraps and have no connection with the production of clothing or the manufacture of other items, most of which are made from plastic not hide, sinew or bone. To many of us, the idea that living respectfully with other-than-human persons might involve killing them, devouring their flesh and utilising their skin, bones and sinews may seem outlandish, even appalling. For our ancestors, it was a vital part of lives in which there were no boundaries between what we now call the practical and the spiritual and far fewer between human and other-than-human people.

In traditional societies there is often a covenant between hunter and hunted, a bargain sealed between our ancestors in a legendary time when boundaries between humans and other animal people were less distinct, communication between the two was easy and shape-shifting common. Rules of behaviour were laid down to ensure the successful continuation of prey species: hunting seasons were set so as to avoid harming pregnant animal persons, young animals and nursing mothers were avoided, numbers killed were limited and remains left after a kill were ceremonially disposed of in rites that ensured the rebirth of the animal person. For their part, animal persons continued to give themselves to the hunters. Sacred songs and dances were given and ceremonies created that reinforced the covenant through regularly recalling and re-enacting it. In them, humans took on other-than-human identities, partly through donning masks and costumes that conferred other-than-human appearance on them. So dressed, they sang spirit songs and danced mimicking the movements of animal persons. Songs and dances were invariably gifted to humans by animal persons. Although I write in the past tense, there are still cultures in which the covenant has been maintained and, as we shall see, others in which it is being renewed.

Ceremonies through which the covenant was sustained often featured not only prey animals but fellow hunters, notably Wolf people. Wolves were rarely hunted by humans. Rather they were seen as teachers. Our ancestors observed Wolves' hunting techniques and how Wolf packs cooperate, sharing responsibilities and rewards. They observed the covenant operating between Wolves and their prey, seeing how, for example, an ageing Stag would often break away from a herd, offering himself to the hunters so that the rest of his tribe may live.

The Bible was instrumental in breaking this ancient covenant. Genesis 1: 28 says that, "God blessed them [i.e. Adam and Eve], and God said unto them, Be fruitful, and multiply, and replenish the earth, and subdue it: and have dominion over the fish of the sea, and over the fowl of the air, and over every living thing that moveth upon the earth" [my emphasis]. This places humankind in a category separate from, and superior to, all other living beings. Genesis 9: 2 repeats this and adds that, "the fear of you [i.e. Noah and his family] and the dread of you shall be upon every beast of the earth, and upon every fowl of the air, upon all that moveth upon the earth, and upon all the fishes of the sea." In the Bible, Wolves are no longer teachers and exemplars but destructive, ravenous killers. So, rather than kinfolk worthy of respect and reverence, the Abrahamic God presents animal persons as a resource for humans to exploit or a danger to be feared.

Restricting the concept of kinship to humanity is problematic for many of us, for many reasons. I never felt I belonged in the human family into which I was born or among the children I went to school with. Attempts to relate to them left me frustrated and upset to the point of overwhelming grief. By contrast, I felt a strong sense of kindred with the semi-feral Cats for whom my mother put out food, the Gulls who wheeled and screamed on the beach at sunset, a lone Heron who stood at the side of one of the dykes criss-crossing the flat fields on the edge of Romney Marsh where I grew up. Any contentment I knew as a child was found roaming the fields at night with the Cats, walking the seashore with the Gulls or imagining myself as the Heron. We refer to these things as belonging to 'the natural world,' implying that human society is somehow unnatural, which is exactly how it seemed to me.

Nevertheless, my human form required me to inhabit the human world and I tried to find kinship in it. For a brief period in the late 1960s, *Homo Sapiens* seemed on the verge of becoming wise. This global revolution reached its peak in 1967's Summer of Love, when peace seemed about to put an end to war and bring people together in creative cooperation and joyous celebration. The following year, this blissful season of hope was clubbed, tear-gassed, water-cannoned and shot to death by armies and police forces worldwide. Some of us strove to keep the dream alive. Part of my reason for founding the British Druid Order (BDO) in the 1970s was that if I couldn't find a human community where I belonged, maybe I could create one.

My other-than-human relationships expanded dramatically in 1994 through a ceremony led by Georgien Wybenga, a wise, gentle spiritual teacher from the Netherlands. During the rite, a full-grown Wolf appeared to me and I left my body, following him to the edge of a forest. He told me his name and that when we met again, he would lead me deeper into the forest. He became my guide, teacher and, through shape-shifting, my alter-ego. Through him I have the craft name, Greywolf. Eight days after our first meeting, I was given a rug made from the hides of six young Wolves. Not long after this, I was invited to a venison feast during which they came to life, becoming a pack for myself and 'my' Wolf. I was given a Wolf tooth for a necklace, a Wolf tail and a Wolf spirit song. These and many other gifts marked my adoption into the Wolf tribe.

Around this time, I started working with a Bobcat who, in human form, is called Emma Restall Orr. She joined me as joint chief of the BDO in 1995. By the end of the millennium, the BDO was one of the largest Druid groups in the world and my dream of creating a human community where I belonged had become a reality. Then, in 2000, my wife, Ellie, died after a two-year battle with leukaemia and I found myself a single parent to our children, then aged six and eight. This, and a series of unedifying squabbles between Druid groups, led me to reassess my relationship with the Druid community. For a decade, I had devoted around 40 hours a week to it with virtually no financial reward and very little thanks, so in 2002 I decided to close the BDO to focus on my kids. To my surprise, messages of support arrived from people saying they would continue to consider themselves members of the Order. Most poignant of all, my kids said the same.

So I retired. The Wolf tribe, however, had other ideas.

On a visit to the US with my kids two years later, friends in Seattle arranged for us to spend a night on an Indian reservation. Neither they nor we knew anything about the tribe other than that they rented out cabins on the Pacific coastline. To get to the res, Ani drove us through the Olympic Peninsula's temperate rain forest. It lived up to its name, raining the whole way until we came within view of the ocean, when the sun broke through. At the tribal village, we checked in to pick up our keys and were told we should go to the village hall where a potlatch feast was about to start. We had no idea we would be there on the one night of the week when the potlatch was held. Arriving at the hall, we were shown to seats and brought plates of delicious, fresh-cooked Salmon.

When everyone had eaten, the tables were removed, chairs pushed back against the walls and it was announced that a drum circle was about to begin. Again, we had no idea this was going to happen, but I had with me a drum I'd bought in Seattle the day before. Vince Penn, the MC for the evening, said "It's the tradition of our people that the person who comes from furthest away gets to speak first in our ceremony..." He was walking in my direction as he spoke and concluded, "... and that's you."

I felt I had to say something but had no idea what, so stepped forward and said, "My name is Philip, also known as Greywolf." All I could think of to do then was sing the Wolf song I'd been given amongst the old stones of the Avebury henge. It starts slow and builds to a crescendo where you can't drum or sing any faster and start howling instead. I did that. When I stopped, there was a brief silence followed by a round of applause. The ceremony continued with tribal members giving gifts to friends and neighbours who had been good to them and little gifts distributed to children. My kids seemed to get more than most. Vince then announced that the tribal elders had agreed I should be made a member of the drum circle and gave me a t-shirt bearing an image given to one of the group in a vision. I joined in the drumming for the dances that followed, in which my kids were encouraged to join. As the evening drew to a close, Vince told me his wife wanted to talk to me and my kids at her office next morning. My experience of being called to offices was mostly at school after being accused of a misdemeanour so I worried we'd broken some tribal protocol, although everyone seemed really friendly.

Next morning Ani drove us through the village looking for the tribal offices. Everyone we passed smiled and waved, which was encouraging. In her office Sharon explained that, five days earlier, the weekly meeting of tribal elders had taken place. The first few arrivals were taken aback when the next didn't say hello but asked loudly, "Where's Greywolf?" They said, "We don't know a Greywolf. Do you mean Grey Eagle? He ain't here yet." "No," he said, "it's Greywolf, and he's either here or he's comin'." When I stepped into the circle and said my name was Greywolf, I hadn't noticed the tribal elders all looking at each other. Years later I learned that my part in the ceremony was the subject of discussion among the tribe for weeks after.

The tribe in question is the Quileute. They trace their descent from shape-shifted Wolves. K'Wati, the Transformer, travelled around the Pacific Northwest teaching the tribes what they needed to live. He showed the Makah how to hunt Whales, the forest tribes how to forage and hunt Deer and so on. Reaching the Quileute land, he found no humans but many Wolves, so he changed two of them into humans and they are the ancestors of the Quileute. Their origin as Wolves makes the people strong and brave. When I stepped into the circle and sang my Wolf song I knew none of this, but Wolf spirit did.

That ceremony came at just the right time. Having spent a decade leading ceremonies for up to a thousand people at each of the eight major Pagan festivals at sites including Avebury and Stonehenge, I stopped attending any rites in 2002. The Quileute drum circle was the first ceremony I'd taken part in for two years. It was very different from those I'd been used to, involving the entire community, beginning with a feast, featuring drums and dancing, masks and costumes, all of which were rarities in the UK at the time. It was more engaging on every level than the usual Pagan rite, which often consisted of standing around in circles speaking prepared speeches from scripts.

Through Wolf, I found kinship among the Quileute.

Like most Indian peoples, the Quileute have experienced the suppression of their culture, language and spirituality by European-American authorities. Living in the far reaches of the Pacific Northwest, they were more fortunate than most in that European-

Homecoming

American influence reached them late and didn't impact them greatly at first. This meant that when they wanted to revive their traditions, there were still some living who remembered the old songs, stories and ceremonies well enough to teach them to a new generation. On subsequent visits I've seen the evolution of the drum circle, with more traditional songs brought in, symbols of the four directions painted on the floor of the hall in which dances take place and traditional costumes made for dancers to dance as Raven, Wolf, Orca and other animal persons. The more traditional elements have come back, the more powerful the rites have become. It has been a privilege to witness this. It also rekindled the desire I had on first becoming a Druid in the 1970s to restore modern Druidry to something like the power it had in its heyday 2,000 years ago. It led directly to the revival of the British Druid Order and to my starting work on its distance learning courses that have been my primary focus for the last 17 years.

I see the BDO's aim to restore our ancestral spirituality as having clear parallels with what the Quileute and other indigenous peoples around the world are doing. Graham Harvey has witnessed a similar revival among the Mi'kmaq of Eastern Canada. Located on the Atlantic seaboard, they came into contact with Europeans centuries before the Quileute, thereby suffering earlier and more thorough cultural suppression. The present-day revival of Mi'kmaq language, culture and spirituality has drawn on detailed accounts recorded by Europeans in the 17th century. Siberian shamanism suffered suppression by Buddhist and Christian missionaries, then by Soviet authorities. Its modern-day revival draws on ethnographic records in Russian libraries and teachers from the California-based Foundation for Shamanic Studies, founded by American anthropologist, Michael Harner. Our revival of Druidry similarly draws on all available sources, from ancient archaeology to modern Paganism. It has the same aim; to restore our native spirituality and culture as part of a process of restoring agency and power to our communities. We feel a kinship with all those worldwide engaged in similar programs of recovery and restoration.

Underlying all such efforts is the re-expansion of our definition of kinship to embrace the other-than-human. For me, Wolves are central. For others, it's Bears, notably the Bear Tribe, founded in 2007 by Kate Fletcher and Corwen ap Broch. Other friends work with Raven, Horse or other animal people or with plant allies. The relationships we forge with these beings are complex, profound, sometimes problematic but, given the threat human activity now poses to all life on our planet through pollution, greed, exploitation and warfare, renewing this kinship and the ancient covenant between human and other-than-human has taken on a new sense of urgency. For us as modern Pagans, Druids, Heathens, Wiccans et al, as for the Quileute, Mi'kmaq, Siberian shamans, Sami noaidi and indigenous peoples worldwide, animism is not a philosophical system but, as it was for our ancestors, a survival necessity based on respect and yes, on kinship.

Homecoming

Kinfolks: A Thought
Gordon MacLellan

Kin for me is a bit like the Indigenous theme we were writing about in Homecoming 1: it is about belonging. That sense of an "indigenous" identity often works on a wide, landscape scale, while the sense of belonging that comes with recognising kin is more intimate. Kinship for me is about acknowledging cousins.

There are so many variations on that teaching "all my relations" that the phrase is almost over-used. It does still feel relevant and apposite, but it is also used almost dismissively. "All my relations" as if saying that makes it so, as if saying it means we're acknowledging it, living it. It doesn't. Being "related" takes work. Families take work. They may be the place where you should feel accepted, that you can always go back to, where the love is unconditional, but that doesn't always happen and it isn't automatic. Growing up as both gay and pagan, I grew used to recognising other kinships. While my family were accepting, other friends were not so lucky and we knew that we were becoming our own family. We gave each other that physical, emotional and spiritual refuge that "family", that kinship, should offer.

Kinship also implies a wider connection than immediate family. This "kin" includes friends, family, who are tree, who are stone, who is a cave, who is a gritstone ridge, who are animal, who are wholly spirit and have no physical form. For me, recognising kin can include just about anything. It is unpredictable. The recognition is not judgemental: we don't admit or reject people because we do or do not "approve" of them. The kin who are part of my spiritual family simply walk in. Some stay. Some keep walking. Some pause for a rest and recuperation and then move on: maybe they're not our kin. Hopefully, there is a family waiting somewhere for those others, but there is a core that holds together.

Homecoming

A Fascination of Toads

People often ask "so what is it with you and toads, anyway?" Or words to that effect. My answers tend to wander, partly because there are too many of them.

I might offer an answer that draws from early, early memories (4 years old perhaps) and determinedly Going To The Pond and the ongoing excitement of heading home with a jar full of tadpoles. A simple excitement of tadpoles. Of their wriggling enthusiasm for life, their shape, their transformation. Then there are seasons of pond visits, of successes and failures before being confident about raising froglets and toadlets to release size....

That answer is true.

There is a more scientific response. I'm a zoologist, an ecologist, and toads are fascinating. Their role within ecosystems is much subtler than just being steadfast predators who sit there and eat anything they can fit in their mouths. Amphibian evolution as a whole is a success story for the underdog. They have crept, hopped, and slithered their way past dinosaurs and extinctions and ice ages. They have worked with their biologies so that, yes, most are bound to water and the spilling of spawn, but others can thrive in deserts, others can give birth to live young. They have explored ways of raising offspring that makes mammalian systems look positively unimaginative. Incubate eggs in your stomach. Embed eggs in a parent's back. Wrap them in strings round your back legs and carry them. Stuff them into a pouch. Lay them in a foam nest above the water the tadpoles will drop into. Lay them in a deep tunnel. Withhold them and let young salamanders slip out later. Or just explore toxicity in ways full of intrigue, hallucination and death. What amazing animals!

Then there is the response from my storyteller, folklorist side, of enchanted frogs, of disenchanted princes, of the Vietnamese Toad who confronted the Emperor of Heaven, gained rain and a voice to sing to the sky. There are toad charms for warts and jealousy and anger. There is Todman, the Toadman, the holder of the Horseman's Word. There is Shakespeare, and woodcuts of witches' familiars. There is the magic of the toadstone that sits

15

inside a toad's head (the rest of us just say, "look! The jewels in a toad's head are those golden eyes that watch the world").

All of those are also true.

There is even a simple aesthetic reply. To me (at least), toads are beautiful. I love their lumpy shapes, their smiling faces. Those golden eyes. I love the lines of a frog and the precision of amphibian toes. The flickering flutter of a courting newt's tail. Beautiful.

Then there are deeper answers that don't always make sense to other people and so are really the ones that matter most to me.

I am an animist. For me, the quality I call spirit is found throughout the world. We all sing in different voices but all sing with the same wonder. We are all connected, all related, both ecologically and spiritually. I have a toad totem. There is a connection between myself and toads (and other amphibians but toad most of all). There is a (metaphorical) toad who sits inside of me, whose presence completes me. Not because he/she/it provides qualities I lack particularly. Nor is it a connection based on calculated astrological balances and elemental wotsits. It isn't that I have a Toad Guide or Higher Guardian Angelic Toad or something. It is simpler. Like deep friendships, it doesn't really make sense. It just is. With toads, I am reminded of patience, of the value of just waiting, and watching, and judging the moment to strike. I am reminded of hidden treasures. Of the long stillness of winter dreaming. Of passion. All of which are things I know as a human, anyway, but maybe the toad-view adds a slightly different perspective. Totemic relationships, kinships, don't need to make sense to anyone else. They simply need to be.

I am a pagan animist. For me there are spirits who still walk this world and gods who watch and wait. And comment. And there is Grandmother Toad who is one of the Ancient Ones, who was here, waking underground, shaping herself into life from mud and gold when the trees dreamed of the First Forest and Raven's wings beat the winds into life and woke all the world. Now, with the trees still dreaming of the First Forest, and Raven sweeping the sky with thunderwings, Grandmother Toad is one of the voices who speaks in the dark of the caves of our practice. She is Contemplation and Laughter and Compassion and the rock upon which you can break yourself. She watches. She smiles. She waits.

Homecoming

So, when I pick up a toad stranded in a ditch with nowhere to go, with a slow exhausted death after long hibernation ahead of it and an urgency calling it pondwards, all these answers move within me. I could try to explain it to you, standing there on the bank above me and asking "why are you doing that?" or I can just smile and invite you to pause, to look and recognise wonder in the little cousins who never give up.

Another Kind of Loving

Hands sinking,
More mud than earth,
Handfuls,
Hands full,
Dripping.
On my knees in old furrows,
Wrapped in this field's flesh,
Under the arms of a hedgerow poplar,
Black-barked and bristling,
All lumps and muscle.

Too claggy for ploughs,
Too solid for spades,
Too wet for earth.
Mud-painted, me,
Earthskin, tattooed
With tracks and slots.
Rising like the field awoken,
Hair a mare's nest of twigs and dreams,
Arms growing branches,
Holding antlers,
Turning
Feeling water beneath my feet,
Mud between my toes, oozing,
Grit.
Sand on cold skin.
Wet-cold.
Earth-cold.
Deep-bone, heart-stopping cold.
And the overwhelming feeling is joy.

Homecoming

Whanganui
Nancy N Sidhu

I want to go visit a river, the Whanganui,
But it is a long way off, way to the south and west,
Too far to go, across the ocean, too far.

But I'm thinking I might speak with it,
The New Zealanders having designated it as a person,
As if we humans had exclusive right to personhood.
Well, I guess it is our word for ourselves.
I don't know what rivers call us,
What whales name us, what words coyotes use for us.
Or best, what our gut microbes might deem us.

What do you think has changed for the Whanganui?
Anything? Or is it just amused at the antics
Of this small, awkward mammal?
Probably there is more than that.
The river is wise enough, aware enough, to know,
We easily could dam it, flood it, bury it in concrete.
So personhood is a kind of safety, a reprieve from death
by strangling,
And maybe the river feels gratitude toward
All the two-leggeds who worked hard, with human
passion,
To save the river from their fellows.

Quietly, with no governmental proclamations or laws,
I grant the sparrows out back, personhood.
I grant the rocks scattered around, personhood,
I grant the spiders in crevices in our house,
I grant furry gray tree squirrels.....
And on and on.
Personhood for you all.

Homecoming

Don't laugh at me, I'm doing my best,
Doing my best to hold you with proper respect,
Proper understanding, proper honor.

And I would be honored if you granted me
Riverhood, squirrelhood, rockhood, sparrowhood.
I would try to live up to the demands,
The requirements, of wisdom.

Homecoming

This

Alison Elliott

I ascend the grey wall and continue to the top of the hill and turn and pick up pace down the slope for the last stretch. An appaloosa lifts its head and returns to graze. Ben Lomond's summit rises between the sycamores, oaks and chestnuts which obscure the foreground hills where a sparrow hawk dives into the gorse and swoops victorious, lit by mid-morning light. Chaffinches fly from the fading hawthorn and bramble hedgerow, a wren now and then flits to a higher branch and disappears beneath while ravens perch on anachronistic telephone lines. Not just a run but a joyous celebration of gratitude, alone but for the flora and fauna which allow me to share this space -quieter again now post lockdown. I return to the car park and stretch inconspicuously behind my Mini and beside the field where the mare who allows me to share her life grazes lazily with her herd. As I drive from the livery yard I think how this love of horses brings together every day a community of disparate souls and even in this love of these majestic creatures little is agreed and even less of our daily lives held in common. And beyond the equine interests everyone has their own complex lives, for many this is their happy place even with the tensions and disagreements. And I think about the contradictions and paradoxes of life, my life and those of others; those I share days with because they have horses to look after too but share little else except pleasantries - on a good day.

Heading out of my daily rural fix I weave my way through the village and homeward to this town where I live - that large old post-industrial town with a reputation for delinquency and poverty despite the mansions which stand in testament to its salubrious past, its industrial heritage and its eponymous shawls. Paisley.

It is the council estates I drive past now although renovated and painted in shades of pastel which earn it this reputation, where right to buy pushed people on to the streets and into the hostels and shifted the balance of the franchise between mortgage holders and renters. What a ruse. And even those who only live less than half a dozen miles away think of it as a no-go, a dangerous place, despite its inequalities revealing housing they would be tempted by if they dared to look - had an interest to look - a place which stains you with your living there. But stains are in the eye of the beholder. And I think of that question I was asked today:

Is it a good place to live?

And I wonder how a place becomes this place you call home. How did this place become my home? The place my ancestors have lived for generations. A great, great grandmother who died at thirty-seven of cholera having escaped the famine and whose husband toiled the land like so many who came from Ireland to this once magnet of a place attracted by the work in the booming mills and whose children's feet walked in the furrowed fields picking turnips. And why do many people stay in one place or return to that place or yearn to be in that place, this place that others do not wish to go. How do you become so connected to a place, a place inconsequential to so many, but of every consequence to you? So connected in your soul that when someone asks a question like this. What do you say?

I want to say:

'I have lived in the heart of this post-industrial town, whose history began long before the revolution and is recorded in tomes and law statutes. Whose history lies beneath the stone flags in the ancient Abbey where a Princess lies, Marjory, daughter of Robert the Bruce, who gave birth to a future King by Caesarean section, without pain relief. Here in this abbey in her tomb laid to rest after falling from her horse. And in the depths below the ground a network of tunnels mark an ancient drain of fine construction over seven hundred years old, one of the first of its kind. And not far from there a horse shoe marks the spot of the last witch killed in this place at a crossroads busy now with some who know and some who don't. And a statue stands in the Abbey gardens of a poet who took his own life in the waters of the Hamills where young boys proved their bravado by tailing the linn and where the dark turbulent waters claimed a few souls, some of their names still etched on storm ravaged rocks. And a supermarket stands acknowledging the past with giant framed prints of children working the bobbin machines, whose lungs were wracked with fibres and their lives cut short and who did not know of the children thousands of miles away who worked on plantations to feed the cotton industry, here in this place. Communities of workers who laughed and loved and cried together, met in alleyways and those who survived fell in and out of love and through the ages danced in the halls on a Saturday night together, connected to this place.

And while the mansions stand, philanthropically constructed by the thread mills' owners, it was the ordinary folks' endeavours the weavers, the spinners, the labourers, the poets, who built this place and live on in the souls of those who know and who are connected with this place. And of those who were bought and sold and never set a foot in this place and for whom no laws or no compensation can compensate.

So the question – is this a good place to live?

And I know why they have asked. This place has had bad press in recent years. And no one wants to listen long enough to hear your answer, because it cannot be said in a sentence.

'Oh yes, this is a good place to live.'

After all I have lived here all my life. I want to say:

'I am this place. If you see any good in me…'

You see my heart belongs in this place. So my answer is:

'It's an old town with a rich history. It has faced problems like most towns in the post industrial world. There are good people here and great transport links to Glasgow and Edinburgh.'

Hoping they would understand.

I drive home from the rural location where the question was asked. I drive through housing estates, new and very new. Through areas built for the aspiring middle classes, on the outskirts of this town. Where there are houses and schools which bleed the wealth from the old town. I drive along the motorway and it is a clear day and I see the once famous skyline – a fibonacci of church spires pointed out to me by my father on countless journeys - that a dwindling number appreciate. I see a cloud above the crematorium and think of the souls of my father and generations of kin and friends and their kin now gone but never gone. Souls of kith and kin swirl and commune with souls recently released in the ether of a collective community. This collective echoes histories untold and yet to be told.   They haunt this place.

This place has a soul so ancient it cries in the wind, through the cobbled streets and through the closes and up the stairs and out through the vents or the chimneys and each new death in the obituaries of the local paper adds to this soul making the wind thicker and denser for all to hear and breathe the atoms of the long gone and departed. So connected are those who built this town who came from far and wide to shape it who lived, loved, worked and died here.

So when I am asked is it a good place to stay, I want to ask the souls who lived and worked in this town and yell loudly at the forces that contributed to its decay. That closed the thread mills and the jam factory and the chocolate factory and though the tannery still works they complain of the stench - the forces that made industrial post-industrial. The forces that left shop fronts boarded up, buildings to crumble, parks to grow weeds and children's swings to rust. That pulled communities apart and broke the strength of unity and set souls apart to put the individual first and they just didn't know how to do that because this was a community, families had worked in the mills, young men left school early and learned trades. They had socialism in their souls. They lived in the council house estates and met in the labour clubs. They knew who it was that had made the country's wealth, it wasn't the big guys, it was the combined effort of all the small guys working together and passing on their pride until the source of their pride was ripped from them and they were left in the rubble - the forces that contributed to our freedom cry.

The reluctant decay of the town centre inspired by the ancient abbey and the town hall which stand with pride over the fluorescent river to where the fish have returned and the mute swans and the mallards nest out of sight in the reeds and form an optimistic front to the storms that rage in the alleys intersecting the old tenements now renovated but here, there and everywhere, lying used and still warm, a council worker removes the sharps in the early morning - the evidence of refuge and hallucinogenic relief from the stubborn stain of third generation downward spiralling deprivation.

When I return to my home in this old town on this mild late October afternoon I sit with my home grown and brewed chamomile and I hear a familiar song…

This is my home
Where this blackbird sings
This song he has sung
With the earth's shifting tilt

This home is mine for a while
Where this blackbird sings
Aloft on a branch

Homecoming

Until October is gone

Why is this home
Where this blackbird sings
And another replies
With echoes of his song

This old town survives
Where this blackbird sings still
Where his kin sang for mine
Through the turbulent times
Of an industrial past

So when you ask
While this blackbird sings
Is this a good place to live
Just listen…

Homecoming

House of Sham

Liv Torc

You keep the tv on.
It was on while you were waiting.
It'll be chattering away when I'm gone.
And I don't take it badly,
It's something we can both refer to,
When nouns and adjectives fail,
Like playing linguistic squash in braille.

We battle passively over pointless points -
Stick to neutral Belgium subjects,
Like work, politics, religion, money -
Two witty people unable to be funny.

I'm good, dad, I say.
But my exclamation is more like a smack,
Defiantly defending myself against his predictable pessimism
attack.
And he reaches for his pipe,
and then shrinks back,
Because he doesn't know what to say to me,
And he senses my urgency.
So I push a little button,
Just a little one,
And say something about Mum.

Skeletons jolt and twitch in their tombs,
While discovery literally puts an elephant in the room.
His eyeballs vibrate frantically

Homecoming

Like two stoppers trying to keep in
an Olympic swimming pool of tears.
The stockpiled spoils of 22 years
of not dealing with it.
So I retreat,
because I'm not that strong a swimmer,
and I want to get out before we both drown.

Maybe see you in a month or two, I say.
The 'maybe' stretches the months into years.
I should say,
I'll come back when things change.
But it's been over a decade since you had a furniture rearrange.
The only pictures of me are pre-purity.
And the athletes foot powder I left on the window sill when I was
Thirteen is still there.

You have trapped your happier memories
And not mine under polythene shrink wrap.
I'm surprised you didn't stuff the cat.
But in truth, I haven't dared to check the shed,
And if I have to stay here any longer
In this Mrs Havisham house of sham,
One of us is going to have to be honest -
Or worse, you'll offer to cook.

So after an hour of talking round large animals
I let us both off the hook.
Get up a little too quickly.
Hug you kindly,
And drive away,
Taking with me the million things
I just can't bring myself to say.

Homecoming

Family Bed

Moon doily
Snot sponge
Bum scratcher
Crumb clinger
Full body tantrum flinger
Softly softly tuneless singer
Hum-dinger

This bed is a protest in defiance of sleep
it paddles the shallows when you long to plunge deep

This bed is a jungle with creepers and croaks, it billows and
Belches and emits tornados of smoke
This bed is a rickety raft on a rag rugged river
A boomerang boat on a milk
Splattered sea
This bed is a life form we will one day set free

This bed is a cave where wolves creep, curl up in packs
Of panting Paws to sleep
This bed is a den nestled deep in the earth, it's full of insects and
Mud and the soft blood of birth

It has elbows and knee caps, fuzz swirls of hair, it has wet wipes
And snot stains and toys it won't share

This bed is uncuttable, in a room they can't tax
It's all coughing and cuddles and noses nestled in backs
This bed is a lighthouse when the dark rages outside and tiny feet
Patter from nightmares to snuggle safe at our side

This bed is a handbrake turn
On a budget magic carpet ride
It is cosy and crowded
and shallow and deep

Homecoming

It is desperately tired
But a long way from sleep

This bed is restrictive and hard to stretch out
It has whinging and shhhhing, and flailing about
It has toddlers and babies and breasts leaking life
It has a man hanging helpless, not touching his wife

Our bed was for lovers
Full of sweet sweaty sighs
Stickiness slick on staccato thighs
This bed is for parents
With no chance of parole
It has plundered our faces
And swallowed us whole

So we lie here like batter
Poured into a pan
A crispy fried woman
And a burnt brittle man

This bed is our children
It's me, you, us and it's them
Hanging on in there
And counting to ten

This bed is a journey I am too tired to make, our eyes
Deliberately closed
Even though we are always
Awake

This bed is a blip in a life full of lazing
This bed is disgusting
This bed is AMAZING

A moment
Some seconds
A fistful of time
A memory so liquid
It will spill down the years
To be served up with tea

Homecoming

And my old lady tears

It's my howl
My heart break
My primal Wolf mother's shout
But right now it's cold
and it's mingin'
So I'm going to GET OUT!

Homecoming

A Memorial

Polly Paton-Brown

Today is a wild autumn day, wind and rain are lashing at the windows of the little cedar cabin where I sit to write. Watching the rain dance on the surface of the lake outside my window, I am reminded of another autumn day, almost a year ago. I had driven with my partner to a wet and windy racecourse to meet a man called Rod. Three weeks earlier, Rod had come to the farm to collect the body of our beloved horse Bouncer, who had died that morning. Now we were meeting him again, this time to collect Bouncer's ashes.

As Rod, a kindly man who looked for all the world as if he should be a jockey, prepared to transfer the heavy wicker casket from his car to ours, he asked me how I was coping without my old friend. "Feeling empty?" he said, his eyes full of kindness.

My response was to say, "Don't make me cry."

Smiling gently, he replied, "You probably will," as he passed me Bouncer's last set of shoes.

He was right, of course. About the emptiness and the tears. In the three weeks since Bouncer had left us, the world had forever changed. Looking at the wicker casket, it seemed impossible that such a little thing could hold the physical remains of that huge body. A gentle giant, whose presence had filled so much of my heart for the last twenty plus years, it was hard to believe that he was gone. But, every day the gap was, and still is, there. No more huge head looking over the stable door, mane in disarray, mud hanging off his forelock like beads at the end of dreadlocks. No more thundering of hooves on a windy day as he and the ponies Firefly and Bonnie-Lass ran and bucked in the field, the wind under their tails, whilst the herd matriarch, Wizard- Star, grazed on unperturbed. No more kicking at the door asking, or rather demanding more treats, if I as much as went near the vicinity of the feed room.

I was not alone in feeling the emptiness.

Oh, dear Bouncer, your little herd missed you so in those early months, the herd you were so caring towards. Always looking out

30

for them, herding them away from danger, standing between them and any threat. Bonny-Lass, your nighttime field companion, took to standing by the fence line alongside Manny, a horse in the adjoining field. He and his herd mates had stood there the day your huge body lay still on the grass. Despite the fences separating you, some instinct in them knew your leadership.

In the days following your death, Bonnie-Lass jumped at noises and walked more cautiously. You gave her confidence despite her failing sight, and she was devoted to you. Sometimes, arriving at the barn in the dawn hours, I would find her standing sentinel like over you as you slept. My heart ached watching her walking alone into the field those darkening evenings, her small frame suddenly looking old and forlorn. One day when she lay down in the field for the first time, I was initially pleased to see her taking some rest. Then I realised that out of the huge expanse of field to choose from, she was laying on the spot where you had lain on that last day, the place where we had said goodbye.

Wizard-Star, your soul mate of eighteen years, once so confident and self- possessed, called for the others if they went of sight. During the day she took over the leadership of the herd, driving the ponies back from the gate with flattened ears and well- placed heels. But at night, when I went into her stable to change her rug and hang her night hay, her eyes followed me, and she gave low throaty nickers. It's then that my tears spilled over and as I leant into her, she wrapped her neck around me.

'I know, I know,' she seemed to whisper with her breath and the way she nuzzled my hair.

I am grateful that on that day, Bouncer, as I collected your ashes, I had no inkling that just four months later, Wizard Star would follow you.

When she first came into my life over eighteen years ago, Wizard-Star frightened me. Fierce and feisty in temperament, she was seen as being wild and out of control. I had no idea then, that she was offering me a new model of femininity, where I could learn to set boundaries and stand in my own power.

Wizard-Star insisted that I respond to her in an authentic way, a way that involved listening deeply to my body and offering respect, treating her as an equal. She refused to tolerate methods that were based in the dominance and control so prevalent in traditional horsemanship.

As the years passed, I saw a gentleness emerge in her as countless wounded children walked into our lives through my therapy practice. Even when Wizard -Star was teaching them about boundaries and ways of being in relationship without manipulation or deceit, I saw compassion in her eyes.

I will never forget the day a little girl ran into the barn, a child who refused touch and who never stayed still enough to receive a loving look. That day, Wizard Star licked her all over, soaking her t-shirt with her raspy tongue. When she went to move away, the old mare gave a deep nicker and the child relaxed back into her. The foster carer and I watched with tears wet on our cheeks.

"She is treating her like a foal,' the carer whispered to me.

And she was right. She licked that little one for almost twenty minutes and I watched as the child leaned into her at the end, her small hands running through the mare's thick black mane. That day as she left the barn, the child reached for her foster carer's hand for the first time.

Wizard-Star was no stranger to rage and taught many, including me, to express the powerful emotions that often covered grief. I think of the foal she lost, the way she was used and her talents exploited by those who should have been looking out for her until one day she struck out in rage and was immediately deemed dangerous. But still, week after week, out on a windswept hillside with rooks and ravens calling nearby, this mare bore witness to adolescent boys finding tears instead of violence, she encouraged silent girls to find their voices and traumatised women let go of their pasts and step into the present.

In recent years, our lives had taken on a different pace. Covid meant that the barn was no longer filled with children's chatter. We found an easy rhythm with each other, enjoying each other's company. Plagued by dermatitis caused by an autoimmune disease, she had no reservation in placing her body beside me and lifting her hind leg so that I could scratch around her teats and belly. She embodied her ageing physicality and expressed her needs in a way that encouraged me to do the same.

Then one day in February, Wizard- Star developed colic. Even as I walked her in the field in an attempt to ease the symptoms, a raven circling over our heads, I knew in my heart that she was going to leave. But I didn't want her to go, and I tried to believe that she would recover, as she had so many times before. Indeed, she rallied for a while and the vet suggested that we allow her to follow her instincts to graze. It was an unseasonably warm day and for a few hours she grazed with Bonny-Lass and Firefly by her side. But the colic returned and her eyes sought mine, locking me into her gaze.

"It's time. Are you ready? I can't stay any longer. I have other work to do. You have to let me go."

It was then that I witnessed something I have only seen once before in my thirty-five years of being with horses. Wizard -Star shed tears. It wasn't a case of eyes that were simply watering, these were real tears that left tracks down her cheeks. I knew in those moments that she loved me deeply, she loved my partner and she loved Bonny-Lass and Firefly. That she wanted to stay but had other work to do, work that could only be done from the ancestral realm, alongside Bouncer and all those who had gone before. She loved us, loved me, enough to leave.

Later, taking the ponies out to where Wizard Star lay in the field, I watched them bid her farewell. In turn, both cautiously approached her still body and both kissed her muzzle with such tenderness it broke my heart.

Losing Wizard Star so soon after losing Bouncer was hard for them. Little Firefly developed severe skin infections - a result of the shock, the vet said, to his already compromised immune system. When I returned Bonny-Lass to the field after Wizard-Star's body had been removed, she sniffed the ground and pawed at the dirt for a few moments, snaking her head from side to side as if in confusion or pain. Then suddenly she took off around the field at a frantic gallop neighing and calling, stumbling twice to her knees as she ran, shrieking for her friend.

In the weeks that followed, the ponies fought and bickered, unsure of how to be together without the presence of their elders. But slowly as the days passed, they began to settle into a new rhythm, and as the spring equinox drew close, they could be seen grazing close together or galloping around the field in play.

As for me, I remember the day things began to change. I was riding Firefly. It was the sort of day we British people might describe as miserable or dull. It felt like the landscape was mirroring my feelings. The lack of bright colour, the rain that threatened but never quite appeared. The subdued sounds and the feeling of heaviness in the clouds.

Homecoming

But something happened as Firefly kept walking. Feeling the repetitive 1-2-3-4 of his walk, watching his ears flick this way and that, listening to him inhale the different scents that I wasn't even aware of, helped me embody the moment I was in, to come out of endless replay of recent events. John O'Donahue wrote in *Divine Beauty* that "Animals have a native closeness to the earth and they move in the sure rhythm of this belonging." One thing I was sure of as we wandered the hedgerows was that Firefly's mind was not full of analytical thoughts. As the ride went on, I let myself just be with him and with the land. As I did, something shifted. Instead of feeling alone with my sadness and wanting to avoid seeing it reflected in the environment around me, I felt like I was being held, witnessed. It seemed as if the land itself felt the loss our beloved Bouncer and feisty, beautiful Wizard- Star. The line of silver birch trees along the edge of the path became a guard of honour, witnessing our loss. When a breeze suddenly made them rustle their remaining dry leaves, I imagined they were applauding little Firefly and his bravery at navigating the world without his elders Bouncer and Wizard-Star to protect him.

Some might call it fanciful thinking. Whatever it was, it changed the way I saw things. The colours no longer looked drained and dreary. I could see the subtle hues were offering a respite from the fierce onslaught of emotion that had been a feature of the days since Wizard-Star had left. I experienced being held by the beauty of a landscape. And I was grateful.

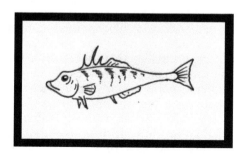

Homecoming

Ash To The Wind

Theresa Kelleher

She stole out in the night. Leaping fences, muffling gate latch, traversing stealthy feet across soft, silent grass. Dragging; grunting; hauling; daring.

They had killed him but she would not allow them his remains.

She had shared so many seasons with him, the bloom and the gloom. The ripeness and the winter's shadow. They'd rejoiced at the hatch of the Collared Doves, the trill of the Robin's morning, shared the acrid black smoke that permeated skin, leaf and lung when the Hoover factory had burnt down.

Against his trunk she had laid her head, sheltered from the beating heat, complete in the knowledge that she could share anything with him. Affairs of the heart were his specialty.

His roots went deep, they would speak through her feet, trunk quivering at her back. And when her ear touched bark a deep resonant song would fill her with all she needed, a wisdom as deep as the forest.

After the felling she wept. Bereft. Heart split as if the axe had struck her too.

Smiling now, as morning brought out angry voices. A missing wood pile. Not a trace.

She gently stroked each severed limb, slowly drying for the sacred time when she would offer him as ash to the wind.

Homecoming

The Garden

Susanne Mathies

Let's take a trip to the garden, our parents always said, not 'to the allotment', certainly not 'to the plot'. In dry weather, Grandpa was in the garden every day, watering and digging and harvesting, shirtsleeves rolled up, baggy pants held up by suspenders, waving at us from behind the red currant bushes: 'Come over here, look what I've got for you!'

Even when it rained, we could often find him there, but then he'd sit in the little house with men from the neighbourhood, and they all drank from small glasses. The smell of schnapps mingled with the taint of mildew from damp furniture and tickled our noses. There were baskets on the table, strawberries or gooseberries, you mustn't pick them too early, otherwise the skin is still tough.

One day he was in hospital. Our parents only said: 'He's not well'. They didn't explain why we never saw him. But we could still come to the garden, the key was hanging on the nail behind the shed above the tarred rain barrel.

Nobody liked to go into the garden then except us children. Our parents had to look after it as long as Grandpa couldn't get up. In autumn the damp was everywhere. The garden was always clammy, even back then when he was still around. He used to construct Red Indian tents for us underneath the quince tree, made of musty Persian rugs and bamboo poles over the green grass. Inside, the space was cramped and dark enough for us to share naughty secrets about the strange children next door.

The tea cups and saucers had rings of grime in the grooved edges, as if a lace petticoat had dragged through the dirt. You could see it clearly, but no one said anything. The cupboard no longer shut properly, and wetness and ants crawled in and left their traces. We never took any of the sugar from the porcelain bowl, but Grandpa just laughed and dipped a cube in his cup, 'It'll take more than that to finish me off!'

He had a fresh pack of biscuits there for us every time, chocolate digestives. You take a bite and suck the chocolate cover off so that the crumbly part can spread sweet and warm over your tongue.

Homecoming

Later, when Grandpa was ill, it was a relief to hang up the key when leaving the garden. There was no time for tea, our parents had done what could be expected. There was no reason to linger.

Sometimes I dream I'm walking down the narrow gravel path again, at the allotment garden colony at Rübenkamp next to the S-Bahn line, past the pale green painted picket fence with the oil paint noses that I couldn't stop because the brush was replete and dripping, but how else would one paint than with a replete and dripping brush?

The garden gate is open, there are new people there. They are decent enough not to show their faces. The door now has a modern security lock. Above the rain barrel, the rusty nail still sticks out of the wall, but there is no key hanging there, only a small round plastic grid on a string, studded with colourful feathers, sign of an unfamiliar childhood that doesn't really belong there.

Homecoming

Cuckoo

Liz Williams

They say: your name is who you are.

They say: change your name and change the world. For the world around you is a fragile thing, a spiderweb in the rain, and even a little tweak can make its tapestry unravel and sink twisting useless to the earth. You know this is true because you have seen it happen, seen the shadows gather, seen the darkness come from an unwise word.

But what if others change your name for you?

A young cuckoo will draw other birds to it, not just its slyly adopted parent. Once it learns to fly, it will perch on branch or stone, mouth gaping, inconsolable. Birds will come and feed it: stonechat and sparrow, linnet and robin, some even perching on its spine to stuff insects into its beak.

I, too, am like this, but it isn't food that they give me. Do birds secretly hate the outsider in their midst? Do they pretend that everything is well? I often wonder. The women of the teulu are sweet to me, at least to my face. They curry my favour, bring me gifts. I was their favourite little girl. But then I became a woman and – well, the sweetness is still there. We are all so happy together. Yet sometimes I see an uneasy glimmer in a companion's eye and I think: do you know?

But know what? I know who my father is, Maredudd, the king of the northern fortress of Penrhynarth, a petty warlord. I know who my mother is, Ceinwen, his wife. Once beautiful, they tell me, lovely and fair just like her name, with shining silken hair that is now wiry and grey around her weathered face, which is marked with a web of veins like red threads. The women of the court remember the night of my birth, the terrible storm, how my mother so nearly died, how thankful they were when my small pale form slid out into the firelight. I nearly died, too; I was not left alone for a moment, the dyn hysbys chanting over us, burning mugwort and hyssop and wild raspberry leaf, cajoling the spirits, calling.

Homecoming

Come, you apple-sweet murmurer, come, you who are honey in the blood, come, and go you lord of the storm, the thunderer, we bless you, pray you go....

There are stories of changelings but there are no such stories of me. That is not my story. So why does everyone call me by such a nickname, Gwcw, cuckoo, when my name is Perweur?

When warriors from other teulu come, I am kept inside, out of sight. I was the one who first insisted on this, and I still bow to it, meek and humble. I say, I do not want to encourage the attention of the warriors. I say, I do not wish to lose my virtue before I wed. Though no-one has mentioned marriage yet, and why not? Matches are being made for other girls and I am the warlord's daughter. There are eligible young men in other households and I have been told all my life that I am lovely. It puzzles me and it gnaws at me at night, even though I do not really want to be wed. And my virtue has long since melted away like snow in sunlight.

The court believe me when I say these things and I am spoiled, up in my chamber, with curds and meats and sweet things brought up while everyone else feasts below. I bow my head again and am seen to be grateful. What they do not know is that I have found a way out. I am slender enough even in human form to fit through the slit of the window, and climb down the rough footholds, sprung with valerian, down to the hill on which our fort is built and then away. Often, I remain alone. I run through the summer meadows, frosted with cow parsley and sunlit with buttercups, or through the frost itself, in winter's decay. I go to the woods and the river, watching the bright stars above or feeling the gale on my face, and I am always back by morning. And sometimes I borrow a form other than my own: the white moon-faced owl as she glides over the meadows, searching for prey. When I do this, when I change, I always think: does someone know? Is this why I have not been promised? But it's more likely that they'd put me to death, if they did know. There are stories about such matters, from the long-ago when things were more fluid. But I also know that it is the compliments they pay me that fuels my power to change, the attention, the admiration, and like the cuckoo, I sup it up and give nothing in return.

Sometimes when I go out I double back, slip through the meadows to the gates of the fort, where the visitor's guard is waiting, and then he, whoever he is, follows me to the woods and we do what we do. They think, after, they have been fairy-led and perhaps they are right. They think they have been dreaming and perhaps they have. They beg me to stay with them, to come away with them. They promise that they will take me south to where the valleys are shallow and the pigs root for acorns in the oak woods and the herds graze by the river's edge. Sometimes I am even tempted, but it would lead to war. So back by morning I always am, when they have fallen into sleep or, fearful that their lord will find them gone, return to their teulu.

But when Gwyr came to the court, things changed.

I knew that the people of the Baedd Tân were coming, of course. It had been planned ever since the winter before, when messengers were sent. They sought a marriage, an alliance with Maredudd's daughter by his first wife, my half sister whose birth had caused her mother's death. Her name was Heulwen, although there was little of sunshine about her. She was not flaxen-haired, nor blue eyed, but as dark as the southern tribes themselves. However, she was undeniably beautiful. We did not get along. I was happy to hear that, if she pleased Sulien, the leader of the Baedd Tân who had lost his first wife a year or so before, that she too would be heading south with the war band, far away. Sun-born and Sunshine: they would make a lovely couple.

Sulien rode into the court one morning in September, when the warmth still lay heavy on the land and the orchards smelled of apples. He first saw Heulwen walking among the trees, with the red, white and black butterflies all about her, and immediately ordered his bard to compose an englyn, about how she, too, was red of lip and white of cheek and black of hair. The bard, I thought, must have been relieved that this was an easy one: Heulwen might have been all light brown and dumpy. Though I suppose there are always wrens to fall back on, or moths. Heulwen, however, was delighted with the bard's efforts and luckily, also, with Sulien himself: a big man, not young but not old either, with a large chestnut beard and a sunny enough smile. I knew the type: genial if things went his way, unpleasant if they did not, and so things usually did. He got on with my father like a podded pair of peas.

I went to my chamber as usual when the warband arrived, with a demure word to my mother, who barely noticed it. She was concentrating on getting Heulwen safely off the premises: sorting out her linens and her woolens and her jewellery. The hunters had been out that morning and shot a brace of deer, stags not being Sulien's grandfather's personal totem or anything ill-omened (we'd checked). But before I went, I had marked the target for my own arrow: a young warrior, as black-browed as Heulwen herself, with straight hair that fell to his shoulders and a dark watchful gaze. I thought he might prove a challenge, but I like those. He looked a little less stupid than my conquests usually are: quite a lot less stupid, in fact. I don't, in fact, prefer stupid men, but let's face it, that was what had proved most available. A little bit of gossip among the maids suggested that his name was Gwyr: one of them had heard another warrior call him by name. Well, I thought to myself, let's see what he does know. It was a thought that I'd later regret.

I myself did not know that he would be on watch that night, but I felt that it could be so. I see snatches of the future sometimes; they do not always come to pass, but many of them do. So I left my chamber by the door, on human feet but owl-quiet, and ran along the top of the courtyard wall. They were all in the great hall, apart from one of Sulien's men who was outside, but too busy vomiting to notice me. When I reached the gateway, I stopped and looked down.

Gwyr was at the gate, looking out over the great fall of the land to the mountains. There was a new moon over Eryri and the distant gleam of the sea under starlight. I did not stop, but ran past him, swift as thought, bat-flitting, down to the marshy ground at the foot of the slope on which the fortress stood, with the stand of oaks beyond. I felt him start as I passed by.

This had been the pattern: I would run by, catch the man's attention in my swift snare, stop, turn, glimmer. Against the dark background of the trees, the image of me was shining pale. I knew how to cast a light. I would smile and beckon; the man would step forwards, faster, faster, as I beguiling led him on. And this was what I expected to happen now, but it did not. Gwyr was suddenly there, a foot away, so close I could have reached out and touched him, almost upon me. But I could not see his face, for I'd had no time to cast that light and his form was cut from darkness.

The shock jolted me. I felt myself change shape, but not into the white winged owl: instead, I became a spire, my roots sinking down into the damp earth, my flowers opening purple as they felt the sun above me. It had been night, but was no longer. My thoughts grew calm and slow. But we were in September now, when the loosestrife

Homecoming

starts to brown and wither, and Gwyr had not gone away. I felt him burst out of the earth, twining, bindweed's green coils strangling the tall spike that was myself. In terror I writhed free, became owl, shot through the trees hooting in panic and daylight, and was out over the meadows. Here I could hide, I thought, he would never find me there. I shed my feathers as quickly as I could and fell to the earth as a seed and was buried.

This lasted a long while. I felt the earth grow cold above me and harden with frost, then the snow came. My thoughts were a dim dream. At the fortress, feast-tide would have come, when the teulu sank into itself, as I myself was doing. Would they wonder where I was? Had they searched for me? But all the time I knew that Gwyr was not far away. I could feel him in the earth, feared that he might find me, sensed him as my enemy. I knew I had made a bad mistake.

But as the year turned the earth became a little warmer, the light above me a little longer. I knew this, although I could not see it. The earth began to drum, an erratic beat, and at first I thought that it was the sound of the spring itself. In a way, I was right: the sound was that of hoofbeats, as the warband ventured out again after the winter snows. And, fuelled by my own hope, I began to grow. I pushed up from the earth as a bud, opening out as celandine into the sun. The world was all colour and sensation and I basked in the light for as long as I could, before I was overshadowed. Why could I not have become yellow-flowered broom, all prickles of my own? I cursed my inexperience. Nettles pushed up beside me, greedy for the sky. Gwyr was in the nettles; I felt the sting of him and soon I withered in the dark that he cast. Travelling down, deep, up once more and the sun sank late in the evening and the land was a-shimmer in early summer. I rose as meadowsweet and this time, bubbling up from the moist soil and under the strong sun, I flourished. It felt like home to me, for we strew meadowsweet on the floors of the fort, to sweeten it. By the time Gwyr found me again, I had flowered into frothy cream. He approached me in insect form, as the great eyed moth and the ghost white moth and the speckled, but he could not sip all the honey from me and I grew stronger, until one twilight I knew that I could take flight again. My fluffy flowers changed to feathers and I flew, and he changed to tawny and pursed me, but I turned on him instead, with outstretched claw and we battled over the shadowy meadows, over the oaks and the stream, and I at last had the best of it and chased him back to where the fort squatted on the hill.

42

Homecoming

He fled from me, as the poet had fled from the mother and maker, as I had from him, into the holes which lie between all things, animal and human and stone and star, as we changed there before the fort to human once again.

As we stood, breathless, on the turf before the fort, I faced Gwyr and as I watched he took on one last shape: his black hair lengthening, his face softening, until a girl stood before me in a warrior's clothes and I was changing, too.

I grinned. My skirts were a bit short for me now. I hadn't been expecting that but I reached out and took her by the hand.
"Come on," I said. 'It's hours yet till morning and the race is not yet run."

Which of us had won? I cannot say. We both found own path between the shapes of things. And we did not speak of what we were or what we might be. We did not speak at all.

When I woke in the grey morning light, Gwyr had gone and I did not see him, or her, among the party that once more rode south, taking Heulwen with them – for although a year had passed for us, following the wheel of the seasons round in our strange long dream, for the people of the fortress it had been just a single night.

But later I discovered that Gwyr had spoken to Sulien, who had sent a message to my father. It seemed that marriage might be on the cards after all.

A happy ending? The strange not-changeling girl and her handsome shape-shifting warrior, whichever was which, together at last? But the bards rarely sing of happy endings, the knots untangled and neatly tied in the handfast bow. Rather they sing of subtlety and shadows, the mist concealing the forms riding from it, that which both is and is not. I had this in mind: I did not want to wed, but I still thought of Gwyr, with wonder as much as desire. Curiosity might have won out but I didn't have a choice. The relief in the faces of my parents told me as much: their cuckoo was finally about to fly from her nest. I dipped my head and murmured that I only wanted to please them.

"Good," bellowed my father, hearty to the last. "That's settled, then! You'll ride south in the spring."

Before that came winter-tide and without Heulwen and her constant sniping, it was pleasant enough. We had hard weather that year, keeping the teulu confined indoors, although I managed to slip out a few times, in the form of the white owl, almost invisible against the snows. I did not feel that I should touch the earth, in case it snared me once again: I could feel all the forms within me, meadowsweet and broom and oak, loosestrife and fireweed and celandine, all the seeds of my spirit.

And what of Gwyr? What had he become, during our separation? I did not love him, I barely knew him, but I no longer feared him, having bested him once, and I remained intrigued. So I rode south, with some of the warband, once the tracks had opened up again.

It was the farthest I had ever been away from home, and in spite of the mud and the chill and the rain, I rejoiced in it. Whatever happened to me later, I would have this memory, of the bright green of the new beech leaves and the bluebells on the heights, of the cloudspun sky and the great expanse of the sea along the bays that are our most western border. We heard my namesakes calling in the woods and the warriors roasted wild pig and venison over the fire at night. Sulien's land was a rich land, one of the warriors told me; I would like it there. A gentler land than the north, though still with high beacon hills, and Sulien's teulu was in a river valley, with good grazing.

Gwyr rode out to meet me with a small party of warriors. He was as I had first seen him and I did wonder briefly if I'd dreamed the whole thing, but I knew I had not. He smiled when he saw me and was courteous and kind. We went into the fort, a strong sandstone place with a great many hens running around underfoot, and were told that the household had killed a cow for the evening's feast. Sulien's old mother took me aside and started babbling about beehives and herds and corn. I made an effort to be charming at dinner, although I felt the weight of Heulwen's disapproving gaze. She would not have wanted me to come but she would have had no say in it, either, so here we went again. She was heavily pregnant by now, though, and retired early. So did I.

They had given me a small chamber in the tower, with a view down the valley, in sight of the great full moon. I slid out through the window and floated down to a boulder on the river shore. I knew Gwyr would find me and so he did, in human guise. It's always easier for men, to slip out at night.

"I'm glad you came," he said.

"Do you truly wish to marry me?" I said, girl again, sitting demurely on the boulder.

"Why not? We both have the same secret."

"Why?" I burst out. "Why are we like this?"

Homecoming

"Freaks or sports," he said. He sat down. "But I think not mules. Maybe like a white blackbird. Just as hounds are bred for speed and sight, so we have been for shifting shape, but accidentally, unless there is some hand on the gwyddbwyll board that is this world, some ancient god moving the pieces about. Perhaps your great-great grandmother was the queen in legend, made of flowers and changed to owl, by a man who was a magician, as my ancestor is said to have been."

"That queen did not bear a child," I said.

"Do we know that?"

I was silent, for we did not.

"I have something to show you," he said, "for as I have said, we are not mules." He reached out and took me by the hand and led me amongst the oaks. There was a path there, a badger track, and we followed it up onto the slopes of the great hill which overlooked the valley. There among the thick groves of blackthorn, with the mass of white blossom that would turn to sloes in the autumn, was a hollow in the earth, and in it was a child.

She was very small, about the size of my thumb. She slept curled in a nest of owl's down. She did not stir but I could see her breathing.

"Sometimes, when I come here, she is just a head of meadowsweet, or acorns," Gwyr said. "Or gorse prickles, like a little hedgehog."

"Did you – bear her?" I whispered. He snorted.

"I don't remember such a thing. I don't think so, or not in the normal way. I was a man again when I left your side, back there in the north."

"I didn't see you go."

"I left before dawn and waited for them down the track. I wanted to be gone." He hesitated. "I was afraid. Of you. I still am afraid."

"I was afraid of you, too. But I think I am more afraid of myself." There was a short pause. "When did you find her?"

"Not long ago. I could feel something, shining on the hillside, beckoning me. I went to see and found her here. But she seems to grow very slowly. And she is nourished by the earth, I believe, when she is a plant."

Another cuckoo. This was not how I had been born: I have told you of that. But when I spoke of it to Gwyr, he told me that he himself was a by-blow of Sulien's, from a woman down the valley,

45

and his mother had not lived long after his birth. He had been taken into the teulu and raised by a wet-nurse. All ordinary enough. So we still had no answers.

The child grew slowly in her nest on the hill. I wedded Gwyr and when after a year or so no child was forthcoming, he rode out one day and with a great show, returned with a little girl whom he had found on the hillside. There was a fuss at first but she was only a girl and the teulu assumed her to be some bastard child, cast away by her mother: how lucky that Gwyr had found her. Some thought that she was his own child, borne to some girl of the valleys. I vowed to raise her as our own, gaining some prestige for my kindness. We named her Genilles, after Gwyr's mother, but to us she will always be Draenog, hedgehog. And so perhaps the bards are wrong with their unhappy endings, for here we live in the sandstone fortress with our hedgehog and when she is a little more grown I will take her into the woods, into the meadows and out upon the hill and show her as best I may the mysteries of meadowsweet and oak and owl. But the tale is not yet told, the race of our lives not yet run, and maybe some day Gwyr and I will have to take our child further, beyond the bounds and the bonds of this world, and seek out our kin in the hollow hills.

Homecoming

Homecoming

Balikbayan

Gareth N Jones

I have always been interested in the choices people make and the events that occur in their lives which leads them to be where they are at any given moment. The big, history defining events that push people around the globe and take away individual agency in the process, to the smaller, but no less significant events that we like to think we have a modicum of control over. In this vein, my presence here in South East Asia is a result of several choices stacked neatly, each one separately leading to the other until suddenly and without realising I am sat in a hotel restaurant a little over 9500 kilometres from the patch of dirt where I was raised.

A Filipino band plays in the corner of the restaurant. They play effortlessly. The five men are skillful musicians and the young woman singing reaches all the right notes at all the right times, but no one is really listening, and the band know it. Filipino entertainers are a common sight around much of Asia. Filipinos also find employment as domestic workers despite often being university graduates or highly skilled in other fields of work. Circumstances bring them here. Circumstances brought me here too.

Filipinos abroad are referred to as balikbayan. The word not only describes their status as part of a diaspora numbering millions, but embedded in the word is the implicit idea that they will one day return. I think there is a poetry and a romance to this. The idea of returning home no matter how far you have travelled or for how long you have been away, is a powerful one. It is an idea of belonging. An idea of a deep connection to the land that bore you and your ancestors which can never be severed. A connection, I visualise as a thread trailing behind me as I travel. Sometimes I feel this thread pull and when it does, I wonder if I have been away too long.

The hotel restaurant the band is playing in is on the Kowloon peninsula, Hong Kong and I am here with another group of balikbayan who have become my family, namely my wife Ryn, her brother Isaac and their grandmother, Ricarda. Ricarda is the only

Homecoming

ethnic Filipino in my wife's ancestry, the rest were Chinese immigrants who fled during the Chinese Civil War, settling far from China and for the most part never returning.

Hong Kong is much colder than on any of my previous visits here. In fact, it is positively bitter. It is the kind of cold that reminds me of the windswept valley I once called home, and of Saturday mornings breathing into my hands to warm them while trying to avoid having a ball kicked at my bare legs as we lost yet another football match. The radio stations say it is the lowest temperature in Hong Kong for a generation. I am convinced that I am feeling the cold more acutely because we have just arrived from the Philippines. Just a few hours before, we had been sitting in the Chinese cemetery in Davao on the southern island of Mindanao, lighting incense and paying respect to those who came before us.

Chinese cemeteries are not like those in the UK, well at least the one in Davao isn't. It is more of a concrete and stone construction with awning protecting us from the sun while we sit. There are marble headstones too, with a pane of glass covering a small recess which houses photographs of the dead. Photographs of my wife's ancestors. There is a notable absentee from the many faces though, that of Ricarda's husband, Cho Boi Go.

Cho might have lived most of his life in Davao, but it was not the place where he wanted it to end. Perhaps he felt the thread pull at him and he realised he needed to return to his ancestral home in China. Although he was someone I never met, I nonetheless feel a connection of sorts and have been intrigued to know more about him. Being here is an attempt to follow in his last footsteps as he returned to China after a life lived elsewhere.

There are not many people in the restaurant and the band take brief hiatus, thanking the room before wandering over to the bar. I am tired from the flight and feeling withdrawn. The conversation around me is conducted in Visayan and as we wait for our meal to be brought to the table, my leg begins shaking - a nervous habit which acts as a lightning rod for my anxiety disorder.

Ryn translates for me, occasionally getting lost in the conversation with Isaac and Ricarda, and I realise much of the content will never reach me. I understand the occasional word as well as names and places weaved into the discussion. Ryn relays snippets she thinks significant.

Not for the first time I am reminded that as with many people from this part of the world, they can converse in several languages with enviable skill. My attempts at French are woeful by comparison and my fragmented Welsh more of a curiosity which they ask me to recite when they want to laugh at the lyrical intonation. All the time spent in the Philippines did little to improve my Visayan beyond a phrase or two since any attempts to use it were scuppered by Filipinos desperate to make use of the opportunity to practice their English. Besides, I fancy have an ear for languages but not a tongue, and Visayan sounds almost entirely composed of glottal stops which I can't replicate without feeling self-conscious. I often feel removed from my surroundings, never quite a part of the events I behold, and I wonder if Cho might have had the same feeling, and this might be something we shared.

Little is known of his life prior to his arrival in the Philippines. No one seems to know what he did or even exactly which part of China he came from, except to say that like so many of those who arrived in the Philippines at the time, he was Hoklo Chinese. This narrows the search a little, likely placing him in Fujian province although piecing together the early part of his life requires a lot of guesswork and assumptions, which while not altogether unreasonable, they are unsatisfying. It is likely that he made his way south towards Hong Kong when the civil war resumed after the Japanese surrender in World War Two. The second phase of the civil war ultimately seen Mao Zedong and the communists take control of the country as the Kuomintang were pushed southward following repeated defeats in battle. Cho's journey appears to follow this chain of defeats although nobody knows if he was a soldier or simply a civilian fleeing the devastation the fighting brought. This part of his story has been lost.

Ricarda does not offer much information and it is questionable if she even knew. Perhaps Cho never talked about it, and it did not matter to her where he was from or what his life was prior to them meeting and their life was built on an idea of a future together rather than what came before. I can understand that point of view.

In any case, it is enough to note that by the time he arrived in Hong Kong, he had already travelled almost 1500 kilometres. As if that wasn't far enough, he then boarded a ship and sailed out into the South China Sea, not knowing if the view back to the harbour would be his last glimpse of China. The more I learn about him, about his story, the more I feel myself wanting a connection with him. I like the enigmatic nature of his life and am drawn to this Steppenwolf, named Cho.

Homecoming

Ricarda suddenly becomes animated, her voice joyful as she talks with Ryn and Isaac. Ryn turns to me, 'She thinks Cho knows that she is here. His spirit knows that she has come to visit him.'

As Ryn translates the gist of the conversation, it transpires that the reason for Ricarda's notion is the inexplicable rocking of a spoon set before her on the table. 'She says it's a sign from Cho. He is letting her know that he is with us too, watching.'

We all watch the spoon, and I have to admit that it is indeed rocking ever so slightly. Ricarda is transfixed. The spoon appears to vibrate with an energy invested in it from somewhere and it is enough to bring a reverential end to the conversation. Ryn reaches across the table and holds Ricarda's hand and smiles are shared. It is a nice idea to think that Cho is here. He had returned to Hong Kong in 1982, so perhaps his spirit is here with us. Again, as with the early part of his life, nobody knows what happened when he returned. He had been diagnosed with pancreatic cancer and while he was still able, he wanted to make the journey back to his homeland.

While Filipinos might have balikbayan, a similar sentiment exists with the Chinese, expressed as ài guó ài xiāng. This is a sense of belonging. Belonging is a basic emotional need, one that pulls and pushes people in all directions as they strive to fulfill it. I believe this explains Cho's return. A return that mirrored his departure; he was alone. What happened next is yet another part of his story that will be lost forever, suitably bookending his life.

Did he stay in Hong Kong? Did he attempt to make it back to Fujian province? When did he die? Where is he buried? As much as I would like to know the answer, these questions do not have any emotional resonance with me. But for Ricarda, I am sure there are many more questions that will go unanswered. His return to China after such a long time had left her alone contemplating the reasons why and quite understandably, Ryn tells me there was resentment on Ricarda's part at his decision to leave and the ill feeling remained for a long time.

Maybe Cho felt the thread pull and he knew he needed to return because his connection to the land was far too strong to resist. This is where I differ from Cho. While I have talked about balikbayan and the Chinese equivalent – I am sure every culture has its version of this – nonetheless I don't share it in the sense it is intended, or the way Cho experienced it. The thread which pulls me is not connected to the land at all. It is connected to a person, Ryn. That is

Homecoming

why I am in the hotel restaurant far from where I grew up. That is why it is not important to me whether I can understand what those around me are saying. That is why no matter where I might find myself in the world, I never feel like a stranger when I am with her. As for belonging or returning, isn't it better to belong with someone than to something? Isn't better to return to someone than return to some place? That's how I feel about it. My connection to Ryn is stronger than a connection to a piece of earth.

Just as suddenly as it began, the movement of the spoon stops. Sometimes not knowing the facts leads us to create our own reasons for why something happened, creating a narrative that suits us and helps us to get through difficult times. Ricarda continues to watch it for a while longer and then says something to Ryn.

'She is saying that she is happy that she came.' Ryn says.

Ricarda seems content. It is with this in mind that I refrain from pointing out that the rocking motion of the spoon came to an end the moment my leg stopped shaking.

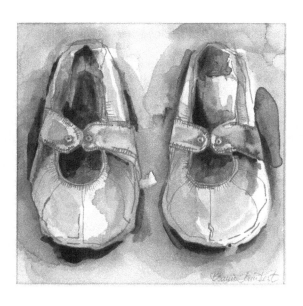

Homecoming

From 'Love Letters to an Alien'

S.V. Wolfland

1) Nightmare or Premonition?

Sweating, an awful sense of struggle - 'Oh my God! She's going to have him killed! She IS! Jesus!' Gasping for breath - 'No! NO!' Oh my God, he's dead - he's not dead is he?' I awake - it's a dream, Jesus H. Christ, that was some nightmare; bolt upright, I am awake, dripping with perspiration, tears running down my face, but so grateful it's not real. I am shaken still though, and am hit with the full realisation of how much I must care about his fate. I tell you, then you ring her - no, everything seems alright.

Five days later, there's a phone call at eight o'clock in the morning - *he's bitten her and she's going to have him killed - she IS going to have him killed, judicial murder!* 'No you're not, we'll have him.' he says at once. She sounds doubtful - 'And what about her?' by which she means me. 'She'll want to have him, I assure you.' he answers. And I do. Very few words need to be exchanged before he's delivered to our doorstep from London the next day. And however I have no idea how this will end, or where he'll end up living, that was so terrible, the thought for one moment that that vital, energetic, conscious, precious-to-himself life could be snuffed out for someone else's convenience? Whatever it takes, he's safe now, he's alive and in one piece, and that's all that matters. Thank God for nightmares. Because of that dream, I had not the slightest shadow of doubt, and now you're safe.

How bizarre - is it even possible you could have sent me that dream, that nightmare somehow? I doubt it. More likely that I was realising how much I cared, and that I was crystallising the fact that I knew that there HAD been trouble with you living where you were, and under conditions I knew which you felt to be unsatisfactory. Maybe even, I was beginning to consider what it would mean or what it would take, for me to offer you sanctuary, or some kind of alternative. I knew these things anyway. But even so, the coincidence and the force of the dream still make me shiver.

Homecoming

2) The Disorganised Games

The meadow was busy with players today, so we went to the weir field, and I caught the edge of your stick, and wrestled you for it with both hands. There we were on the ground, in muddy grass and an icy wind, pulling a branch in tug-o-war, completely absorbed in each other, locked eyes, mine held in your dark gold gaze, and you wrenched and wrenched, and we waited and bided our time for the other to loosen their grip...I could tell you were fully engaged, the remains of your tail at full throttle, your eyes half closed in concentration as my heels dug into the mud, and you write off my jeans, no surprise they're covered in mud with growing holes... You tried to take it by surprise, I gasped; Then grip and haul you toward me with it (as I never could do before) and only after what seems like ages, do my hands tire, and I release first - a kind of draw? But you shred the branch to pieces in victory as I lie energy spent, on the wet grass… Breathing hard, we ignore everything and everyone in these games, totally focussed on the evolving rules and game-pieces and each other...a kind of bond is interweaving around and between us, tightening all the time, and I cannot understand nor can I name it, but a strong thin thread, invisible, holds us in synchronicity on our walks together. You come when I call. I know you can back up your views with teeth. We both know the score. Yet we have a viable and continuing truce, turning itself into an alliance of some sort. Caught up in a phenomena far from telepathy but without any other metaphor, we work out what it means for two radically different species to co-exist in co-operation. Slowly, step by step, we are becoming Tribe. Becoming Pack.

3) The Seventh Time

I

The first time you put your head on my lap, I was surprised and faintly horrified.

The second time you put your head on my lap, I was appalled at how hot, wet and heavy you were,
how much you moulted, the whiff of stagnant water and body oils.

Homecoming

The third time you put your head on my lap, I noticed your eyebrows, the deer-like cut of your chin, got used to the idea of having a plastic bag handy in case you were dripping wet.

The fourth time you put your head on my lap, I felt the beginnings of astonishment at the trust, the intimacy into which I was being drawn, that you seemed to be offering.

The fifth time you put your head on my lap, I found myself accommodating you, trying to make sure you weren't too uncomfortable.

The sixth time you put your head on my lap, I realised that the physical closeness had woven a bond about us, tightened my links to you somehow in some unnameable way.

The seventh time you put your head on my lap, I had seen more fully how beautiful you were. And I fell, irredeemably, in love.

II

And now you sit lolled over me, your heavy but handsome head held in my hands,
and you sit up putting your weight against me, shoulder to shoulder,
and sometimes your head is so close that my lips almost touch your ear...
until I kiss you and you endure it, manfully.

Because now it seems to me that you hardly smell any longer,
just a faint aromatic hint of spice. And your nose is by my cheek,
or your head on my shoulder, and we are so close all jammed up
on this front seat of the van, and I am crazy about you...

Homecoming

4) 'Jaguar - "One who kills as they leap" *

I can't believe it, never thought I'd fall in love with someone like you, never guessed I could be so proud of things that in someone with two legs would be unacceptable. But I understand your differences. It started off as pestilential to me, as I would have to roar at you when you attacked other dogs who had slighted you, when you got into punch ups with aggressive dogs who were trying to take you on or freak you out, when too-friendly or insultingly familiar dogs came up and sniffed you, tried to share the shallows or the watering hole you'd found, and you'd turn on them savagely, with unconcealed temper and menace. Oh how I longed at first to be with someone more calm and collected, more polite and restrained! But how I came to value and understand your temper, to end up always taking your side 'Well they started it.' 'What a bad mannered dog that was, what did he expect?' I came at last to be bizarrely proud of your aggression, because you were always (well, mostly) so gentle with me. At first I looked with horror at the dead rabbit you'd just killed, hanging from your glittering jaws. Then I came to appreciate your skill, speed, daring, and cunning, your efficiency and the way you offered me some, your manners. Then the way you ate it all, like a lion on the savannah with antelope prey. And I finally, to my surprise, fell in love with everything about you. 'Oh yes, he's a hunter - he can catch and kill that, and eat it in ten minutes.' I'd say, blithely. I was one of those who walked with their canine companion no matter what the weather, because you were always up for it, always wanting miles. One of those who walked the less trodden paths, because you didn't like to be with others, didn't want their company or interest. Only wanted me, my attention, my participation and engagement. You won my admiration, it was clear then that you wanted it, and you kept it, truly. I was your sparring partner, playmate, cheerleader, and still am. You claimed my love and loyalty. You were and still are, jealous if my hand touches someone else's fur. But you were Jaguar - 'he who kills as he leaps', with your terrifying, beautiful, exquisite mixture of ballet dancer and killer in one arcing movement. I could wax lyrical over your prowess, your strength, speed, agility, flying leaps, flexibility, and all the wonders of living with a wild hunter and a supreme athlete for two years... But now you have had an operation to mend your ligament, now you have arthritis in your hip and lower spine, now, suddenly you have more patience with other dogs, children, people, none of whom are in any peril any longer, as you know your new limits. You are friendlier now - some of that is trust, since you have lived with us, but some of it is feeling like a 'beta wolf' now. You are more likely to walk with me, not miles ahead, you are more likely to listen to my advice, not just carry on and return to me when you choose. Things have I suppose got easier. You are more what other people call 'biddable'. But I wish you were as you always used to be. Feral, wild, hot headed, fearless, terrifying, howling like a wolf and roaring like a lion, and yet only gentle with me. Like holding a whirlwind barely in check. Me becoming an acolyte of Diana the Huntress who seemed to bless all your exploits whenever we went out together. Until at last I wondered, uplifted, challenged and breathless from running and wrestling with you as I was so often, what was the Wolf God's name? Because it was he I had come to realise, that I wanted to worship, after all.

But now you are different. And yet you are still you. Your dark gold gaze is still clear and bright with extreme intelligence from your large, liquid, beautiful eyes. Still handsome in all you do or say, as always. But you are not Jaguar, not 'he who kills as he leaps'. Nor will you be again. But I will always love you.

5) Last Words

We curl and kneel round you on the floor and weep or try not to weep (it's demoralising for you I should think, no one wants to have mourners before the event).

Shaky and with something weird happening with your eyes, we caress you. I'm so grateful for everything, thank you so much, you've got me through so much, taught me how to live! I can't express how much I owe you...Please, I hope you know I love you, how much I love you, that I'll always love you no matter what...I don't mind what you felt for me, you were so generous in your teaching anyway, it's such a pleasure and a privilege to live with you, it would just mean so much to me if I knew that you knew how much I loved you...' I wonder how you could tell me...? Then, all at once, you lift your head, put your chin in my hand! You've not done this for days! 'Oh thank you!' I cry, tears raining on your pillow...'Thank you so much! That means the world!'

It's all I wanted - to know that you knew.

Homecoming

6) Promises

Two promises I made you - that harm would never come to you when with me - that I would defend you always.

That time the man with two Alsatians started going out with the woman with two Alsatians, on the meadow. The four of them started thinking of themselves as a pack, and one time they were running towards us, towards you. I had read somewhere that you could deflect an attack on the dog you were with by forming a human shield. Even warrior as you were, I thought that four Alsatians bigger than you, made for very bad odds, so I took the plunge, and trusted to them intending to attack you and not me. I crouched on the floor, knelt, asked you to come to me, you did as I asked and I wrapped myself around you. You uncharacteristically stayed, your head covered. They came closer, started to slow. I didn't look at them, hid my face in your fur. They circled us, but didn't attack. Curious and perplexed, they dawdled just long enough for their worried humans who were shouting, to have time to run up to us and drag them all away again. A little shaky, I got up, relieved. You ran off ahead. But I was just a little proud, to have been able to protect you, the way you had done for me.

The second promise I made you, was that (if that time should ever come) if you were ever mortally ill, that you would die in my arms. And you did, I felt your once-powerful, once so lithe and fluid muscular form, now all bones, go lax. All the tension, but also the life. God, how gut wrenching that moment! Graven in my soul. I weep uncontrollably. 'Oh my dear one, I will mourn for you with slightly varying cadence, for the rest of my days.' I choke, paraphrasing the words of a favourite poem*. The vet tries to offer me bereavement counselling. I'm not listening, just hear about it afterwards. My only comfort at this juncture is...that I kept my word.

7) Bereft

Of course my first instincts are of the Wuthering Heights variety - I just want to lie on the moor, hands twined in your fur, weeping till I fall asleep in bracken and grass, stop eating...

Homecoming

But this is Surrey, I can't even get into the wood where you were buried (with agonised love and immense bravery by him) yesterday, (without help) and grand romance doesn't sit well with scratchy difficult ground and ant bites...No, our grand romance, yours and mine is for windswept moors or dizzy mountains...

Anyway our affaire d'amour has left your wolf-wife bereft, my love...feminist as I am, you were the only gendered old fashioned, man I could ever have loved...forgiving you more because I knew that you never forgave humans for being the apex predator (who have screwed up your beautiful birthright of rivers and lakes so royally) even than because of your charms (though I swear you wooed me that summer after you came to us that May).

You came in May - nine years ago?! - he knew you were his right hand man in...June? July? In August you flirted, in September you wooed me, by October I was head over heels in love... and never once looked back.

But (with the cough as well) I have cried so much I have felt like I was drowning in my grief...Today when I walked, it was like wading through treacle...'The gift! The gift of more health he gave you - to bow under this weight is to lose and abuse it! He wouldn't be pleased.' He's right. This dark destructive tunnel won't bring you back my love. Deep breath, count to ten. Try to picture tomorrow and the day after that and the day after that and...

You and I will always be part of each other. Nothing can alter that.

8) A Different Sort of Nightmare

'I wake and go to the bathroom - but I don't have to negotiate or ask or edge round or anything...it's too easy. No being pinned up against the wall. You lair in bathrooms (a water source, and never trusting humans you want to be nearest to it) often, and usually in this room in this house...This inconvenience has always been there in different locations...it's not that or the stress it sometimes involved (it's often driven me crazy) that I miss, but my God, I miss the reason! YOU, your temper, your opinions, your space, your choices, your needs, your decisions, your penchants, your mind, your amazing, thinking, bloody-minded Mind! In You - handsome,

Homecoming

bastardly, bold, charming, loud, proud, opinionated, complicated, crosspatch but still glorious, and adored You!

'Where is he?' Asks the just-risen-from-dreams...'Oh Christ, no!' The morning weep begins and flows...

I miss you so much...

If the reason has left my world I must make a new one...I dance out my grief in the night as if throwing batons for you...seeing you catch and leap and almost fly, in our heydays...*'Jaguar'* I called you then, *'he who kills as he leaps'*...I imagine a dance production trying to express interspecies communication through the Games...I need to create something for you, in memory of you...

I don't know what yet...It won't bring you back to me, but it might send something of your oh-so-burning-bright Spirit, almost-too-hot-to-handle fire out alive into the world, if that makes sense...

9) Suddenly

One day on a journey, it suddenly occurs to me; All the thrilling and glorious memories, all your teachings, the games...some of the best days of my life - I realise in a flash that despite this terrible heartbreak, I'm still so glad you chose me, for the years we spent together. As I always used to sing to you (to your embarrassment) 'You touched me, and I touched the sky, you changed my world...'

In the days that follow there are what I would once have called 'signs'. And it's then that I become more sure that you loved me too.

I guess I couldn't ask for better.

'In honour of the memory of Brân the Blessèd, 28/11/07 - 5/7/23.

Note * the quote is adapted from Geoffrey Hill's 'The Songbook of Sebastian Arrurruz'

Homecoming

Homecoming

Brindle Wing
Carrie Osborne

Wings tilted against the Blue
Catching Sun-glint
The glow of brindle and white underlit in a caress of light
Before curving into shadow.
A languid spiral, effortless,
Turning and turning inward
Until in another heartbeat
She is a speck
Sky-claimed
Far beyond
In a world of Blue

When I was a young woman, swayed in the storm-wracked tides of depression and desolation, I dreamed one night so vivid a dream that it stayed with me across all the years and struggles of my life. The symbols and images of that dream carried me through times of turmoil, helped me rise above intense physical pain, steadied my fears.

I began in darkness, caught in an entangling thicket of thorns, aware of a hunter closing in. I was crow-like, my dark wings constricted and tattered by tearing thorns that trapped me as the hunter drew near.

Dread and panic drove me deeper into the entangling dark, until in my fright at last I broke free, bloodied by thorns, out into a blaze of light.

The hunter took aim as I leapt and took flight, glorious strength lifting me on brindled wings away from the dark lead shrapnel shot. And I rose transformed, a Buzzard exhilarating in the freedom of the winds far from all troubles.

For a time I gloried in the sky, circling up on thermals far, far above, my shadow diminishing from the shackled earth. There was such joy, such unutterable freedom, the pure and savage power of wilderness alive through every vein and feather.

Homecoming

After an ageless time, from my great height with the jewelled land spread far below, I saw a green hilltop and was drawn inexorably to it. I found myself once again in a human form sitting on the edge of that high hill with the land stretching away far below, and gazed out with a feeling of great peace.

But hunters came even to that high sanctuary and I was forced to flee, flinging myself back into the wind, shapeshifting as I leapt once more into a buzzard alive with the elemental power of wilderness.

The dream shifted, as dreams do, and I was human at the base of the hill, earth-mired, stricken. I cried tears of frustration in desperation to regain the summit and the peace of that lost sanctuary. The hill was impossibly steep. The sense of loss overwhelming. My parents were there as I struggled to climb, my mother urging me to pull myself up with her hair. My father's gentle faith in me unwavering.

Another shift, world tilting.

The dream circled to an end with me once more a buzzard gliding effortlessly on the winds, rising on thermals, unfettered and free, and I woke with that feeling of awe still hearing the keening cry pitching on the wind.

Thereafter the presence of the buzzard would stay with me. Visualising the bird circling in a clear blue sky would calm me, detach me from physical pain, give me strength to draw on in my times of darkness and doubt.

To see them, hear them in the wild would make my spirit leap and always awaken that sense of kinship and awe as I watched them spiralling against the blinding sun. They became my totem and my strength.

To feel the wind thrill through me
Feather-clad I rise
Above flickering stormlight
Power over the savage sky is mine.
The winds sharpening desolate crags
Howl beneath my wings
Darkness gathers in the shadow-haunted land
A familiar dread creeping
And yet I rise
On brindled wings
To overcome the gathering storm.

Homecoming

Last summer in one devastating spiral of violence, trauma and death, the world lurched under me.

Waves of panic shadowed my waking days as I struggled to put a shape to the overwhelming storm of feelings that paralysed me like prey. An indrawn breath that I could not let out.

In those first days beyond the shock I dreamed of walking barefoot over shifting shards of glass. They slid sickeningly under my bloodied feet.

There was the strong sense in my mind of an invisible scarlet cord strung taut, reverberating under unbearable tension behind the layers of my subconscious, a constant keening beyond hearing, resonating beneath every waking moment. And the dread of what would happen when that scarlet cord snapped.

And yet day following day with each teetering moment of fright and dread and shock, they were with me. I would look up, become aware of a buzzard tipping her wings to the sun or hear the forlorn cry tilting on the wind. See distant brindled wings circling, spinning slowly against the blue. I felt them with me, lifting me up, as if watching over me, guiding me from the entangling darkness.

Feeling caught in the thorns of anxiety
I looked up, heart faltering
And saw the sun blaze on brindled wings
Three Buzzards lifting
Circling above my home
Guardians of my heart
That even in my fearfulness, lent me strength.

And strength comes when it's needed, moment by moment, breath by breath, my heart wrapped tenderly in barred brindle feathers. As the shockwaves receded and the old year turned on its axis, with the winter Solstice I learned that I needed an urgent major surgery. Another life changing shift to sweep me along while I still reeled from the summer's devastating sorrows. I could no longer flinch from confronting the dread of mortality. I hid the depths of my fears from my loved ones as they hid their own from me. Tremulously I turned to face it, held that indrawn breath.

A sliding terror
A flinching away

Homecoming

The darkness at the edges that turns the blood to ice
And the heart to tremble like prey.
A creeping dread
Blackening inch by inch up the spine
Until like prey breaking cover
I flee those trembling thoughts
Refuse them utterly in my fright.

A chemical sleep
So deep I will not feel the cut of the knife
And what if I never wake?
Will I find my way back from formless darkness?
Fears of mortality crowd
Fluttering fitfully in breathless premonitions
The familiar dread
Urging itself to be heard
And not fled from.

And yet in the cold terror of the operating theatre with the needles and blinding light, I summoned desperately my circling buzzards to lift me up into blue skies and clean wild winds. Surrendering my trust to them, to guide me back from that chemical sleep, so frighteningly death-like.

And later, in the recovery ward struggling through medicated nausea and pain, my defences in tatters, finally the scarlet cord still darkly strung taut at the back of my consciousness, snapped.

It was the Buzzard's cry that brought me back.

That drew me up, resurfacing from waves of devastating panic and pain.

They flew with me all through the long slow weeks of my recovery, on into the spring, as step by tentative step I rebuilt my strength.

I dreamt of a powerful bolt of lightning striking the earth close by me in a dark and rising wind. I felt no fear but leapt up to avoid the riptide of the lightning's power as it surged sizzling along the black afflicted ground.

I was safe.

Between wind and sun
Pain and death and boundless freedom
Between talon and hooked thought

Homecoming

Poised effortless over emptiness
Bright eye
Brindle-wing
Sky heart soaring
Wilderness weaver of winds

Stir me from the clinging dark
To shed this dragging cloak of shadows entangling my every step,
And rise on the spiralling winds.
Let the wind scythe through me
Lay me bare to the bone
Hollowed out
Scarred

The world encompassed in sharp amber eye
Wind-warped light wielded
In curving talon
Horizon transfixed on hurtling axis
Feather and claw
Wilderness in my throat
A skirl resounding sorrow on the rising storm
Lightning shivers my blood
The wind in my bones resonates
Sky dancing
In savage joy
And tenderest bittersweet pain.

Homecoming

A Question

Helen Compton

Question ~ What are roots?

This question started to germinate as inexpressible love swelled within me with each surge of the surf, standing barefoot on Pensarn Beach, unable to either contain or speak my overwhelming love for him, my father ocean ('he' would have no words for 'he', ocean is ocean with ocean feelings and energies and seaweed tangles and razor reefs). I am not of this land; no singing Welsh blood runs in my veins, only churlish Yorkshire muddy rivers. So how do I feel green-silver roots sprouting and writhing from my spirit feet to the grey-green land the second I set foot here? Why do I belong *here* and not *there? And what is belonging?*

Answer ~ Passionate, no, besotted connection with the landscape.

This answer ripened and fruited sitting in the truth of the moors, listening to the surge of water flowing with a gurgling chunter among Ilkley stones. I know this place to be wild and beautiful but it does not make my heart burst with more love than a hormonal adolescent in the fire of first infatuation; I don't crave it, nor feel a tearing grief when I must leave it. I believe I was meant to find this connection with the living Welsh landscape, that something in the land seeks something in the human, though why or how remains elusive. Indeed, why should this romance between land person and human person be different to that between human persons? We cannot define why this individual makes our heart intone loving notes, while that, objectively and equally beautiful person, leaves a romantic silence in us; whether woman or woodland, man or mountain, or any configuration in between, love is mysterious.

You don't have to be born to it, you cannot create it (though you can absolutely listen for it if you can still your mind and your 'I must' long enough). Kinship will arise when you are in the right place and possibly, at the right time.

67

Homecoming

My Grandmother's Shoes
Boann Lambert

My Grandmother's Shoes is a dedication to our matriarchal line of Grandmothers, the wise Women, the Crones. With the ageless *witsdom* of our Grandmothers we can truly find a connection to the earth, a connection to the old ways. We can sew our stitches, make our clothes, and sow the seeds that will feed our future.

She walked a thousand miles
A path worn smooth
by her naked feet,
a journey of grief and joy
and with each step she held
me, deep within her body.
She was waiting
for the day my mother was born,
already seeing her Granddaughter
in her daughter's arms,
the greatest gift
she could ever give.

WITH EACH STITCH, I SAY A PRAYER.
WITH EACH MARK I MAKE, I MAKE A BLESSING.
WITH EACH BREATH I TAKE, I REMEMBER.

Homecoming

Afterword
Jack Wolf

In this issue of Homecoming, we have chosen to explore the idea of kinship. Some of the writers featured, such as performance poet Liv Torc, have chosen to focus on kinship between People – the close ties of love and blood that bind one Human being to another, and sometimes bring joy, sometimes hurt. Liz Williams broadens this concept in her mythologically inspired story 'Cuckoo' in which the boundaries of Human and non-Human become fluid, and the specifics of blood relationships harder to determine.

One consequence of entering into relationship with a Being of any kind is love – and while the other side of love is often grief – evoked in Theresa Kelleher's poem 'Ash to the Wind' – a love relationship with a being that is entirely other can bring unexpected benefits to the Human side of that relationship, sparking new levels of self-awareness as in Helen Compton's 'A Question'. In their elegiac pieces 'A Memorial' and 'From: Letters to An Alien', Polly Paton Brown and S.V Wolfland explore how it is possible to form close familial bonds with non-Human animals, and movingly evoke the grief that is felt when these bonds are broken as well as the enduring gifts they have received from these relationships. Philip Shallcrass, Gordon MacLellan, and Carrie Osborne describe relationships with animals that extend into the realms of Spirits, describing how a non-Human animal can begin to feel part of one's own, Human, identity. Alison Elliott, in her celebration of Paisley: 'This' takes a different approach, describing the way in which places and people are often closely intertwined, and towns are not so much inhabited by people as composed out of them, so that the relationship between architecture and community can be deeper and more reciprocal than it may appear to an outsider. Gareth N. Jones, in 'Balikbayan' explores how moving from one's place of birth can give rise to a profound sense of dislocation, and how finding a new kinship with others can mitigate this. Conversely, in ' A Garden' Susanne Mathies explores how strong ties between a beloved Human person and a particular place can give rise to feelings of alienation from both place and self when those ties are broken – as if the place and person were always, in some sense, interchangeable.

This porous sense of kinship, in which the ties of responsibility and reciprocity that come with being kin extend beyond the immediate family is, as The Dine academic Lyla June Johnson explains, one key characteristic of an indigenous relationship between people and land that distinguishes it from the ownership model that typifies modern habits of land-use. People, the Land, and all its other-than-Human inhabitants are all considered to be, in some way, related. This relationship is no romantic ideal, neither is it some kind of anthropomorphic fallacy, despite the centrality of the Human derived kinship metaphor. In a societal system such as that of the Dine, within which responsibilities to others are of primary importance, blood relationships are not only thing that must be taken into account when considering the duties a Human being has to his or her community – the well-being of the place itself is important, too, as is that of the other-than-human kindred currently living in it, and all those beings, dead and unborn, who have ties to it. If all Beings are kin, all are connected, and all have responsibilities and rights: the well-being of one will enhance the good of all. The fact that some of these Beings may be entirely other makes their well-being neither less nor more valuable than that of the Human community.

This is a notion of kinship that is both far reaching and deeply complex, being both metaphor and social reality; but it is not as alien to modern ways of thinking as might appear. As scientific disciplines from medicine to ecology to climate science keep pointing out, within any complex system, everything has an effect on everything else. Reality operates as a complex, connected system. Replace the words 'complex, connected system' with 'kinship network' and the scientific idea suggests itself as a modern version of an ancient concept.

There is one key difference, of course: the idea of Personhood. True kinship with a Being entails the Personhood of that Being – an idea introduced in Nancy N. Sidhu's poem 'Whanganui'. And while most of us might be able to agree that a beloved Dog or Horse – or even a Toad – is a Person in their own right, it is typically an imaginative stretch to take the idea any further. Can we really consider that the same thing might be true for a River as for a Horse? How can a thing that seems, according to our established definitions of life / unlife, to be inanimate, a thing with indeterminate boundaries (where does a River begin and end?) be accorded any sort of Personhood?

There are several ways of dealing with this conundrum. One is to draw a line somewhere – probably between the creature and the River – and to deny Personhood to those entities who do not have whatever characteristics we have decided Personhood requires. There is is, of course, a logical appeal to this, but drawing such a line has a number of serious downsides – not least that of extracting the living Being – say a Toad, or a Buzzard, or a Wolf – from the ecosystem within which they are intimately enmeshed. A wild Wolf in captivity is still a Wolf – but because they can no longer operate in the wild world as Wolf, how much of their essential nature is compromised – or, at best, obscured? Depending on how important we think this is, it may not really make sense for us to think of Wolf without thinking also of his role within the web of relationships that sustain his ecosystem. Perhaps the truth is that while our individual Wolf may be a Person in his own right, he is also part of a Kinship Network that comprises the whole Ecosystem and every other Being that lives within it? And, taking this idea farther, it may be impossible, both practically and philosophically, to separate one from the other, because the most important thing is, in fact, the ecosystemic Network. Evidence from Yellowstone National Park in the US, where the return of Wolves after seventy five years ultimately resulted in changes to the path of the rivers, goes some way towards supporting this. From a certain point of view, it could be argued that the Being of the Rivers begins and ends within the Wolf: the Wolf's begins and ends within the Ecosystem. Allow Personhood to one part of an intimately connected system, and, logically, you must grant it to all the others.

This suggests that one way forward for most Western thinkers could be to accept that all things that can exist in relationship are also Persons, in ways that need not resemble modern notions of Personhood at all. And as it turns out, the decision to grant legal Personhood to the Whanganui drew in large part on Indigenous arguments that considered it an indivisible and living Ancestral Being. As a different sort of entity, the Whanganui did not need to display the characteristics – such as individuality or consistency of identity – that make Personhood so easy to recognise in a Dog, a Horse, or a Human being. Personhood can be applied in a flexible way that can reflect the complex and unboundaried nature of reality. Kinship can extend to Persons beyond immediate blood

Homecoming

kin, beyond species, beyond form, beyond divisibility or addition, and even beyond apparent differences in Animacy.

But while this consideration perhaps takes us some way into a way of thinking that might not be unfamiliar to the Dine, it remains easier to understand the idea of kinship with everything and everyone when the idea is referenced to a clear and obvious system, such as a Town, an Ecosystem, a Family. How can we incorporate the ideas of Personhood and relationship into our thinking and acting when we consider much less accessible entities such as individual Stones or Oxygen molecules – or such vast and distant entities as the Sun? What about the Universe itself? Does it, or could it, have a kind of Personhood? For many modern people in the post-industrial West, this seems a step too far.

The question is, of course, not remotely new. One way of answering it, at least in regard to the Sun and Universe itself, is to do what many traditional, long established, or pre-modern societies plus some modern religious thinkers have done: answer with an unequivocal 'yes' and name the Being concerned a God. But theologies, whether old or new, are not the only modes of thinking to offer a solution – and very few people would be likely to want to call a beach pebble a God, so this answer will not do for smaller things. Once again, modern science gives us a hint of a way forward – and funnily enough, it is one that leads us right back where we started. Our present scientific understanding of gravity is that everything that has mass is influenced by – and is thus in relationship with – everything else. While a Stone is being pulled towards the Earth, it is also pulling the Earth toward it. This is true of both small and much larger things.

It is easier to see the effect in space. Astronauts carrying out repairs to the outside of the ISS find themselves surrounded by tiny clouds of particles whose gravitational effect, though minuscule, is not zero, while the whole ISS and everyone on it is subject to the gravitational forces of the Earth, Moon, Sun and even the far off Moons of Jupiter. In space, everything from the macro-structure of Galaxies to the behaviour of a lump of junk is visibly in affective relationship with the energies that surround it. Everything is in motion, reciprocation, and ever shifting balance. In a profound sense, it can be said that what the study of space makes visible is that the physical world is created out of relationships more than it is made from matter. If this is true, then within a conceptual system where Personhood is created out of being in relationship, then of course a Stone, of course an Oxygen molecule becomes a Person – though one so radically different from ourselves that any experience it may have of existence is almost unimaginable to us.

But if a relationship carries rights and responsibilities, what can the Human side expect from the non-Human partner when that partner is Stone, or Oxygen? One answer here, I think, lies in the natures of the things themselves: the primary responsibility of Stone is to be a substrate for the living world to exist upon; that of Oxygen to continue to be breathable air for organisms that have evolved to be dependent upon it. If everything is kin, then Air and Stone are, in a way, our aged great-grandparents; having had a generative role at the start, their responsibilities to their children are now very much simpler than their children's are to them.

There is nothing mysterious, 'primitive', or 'woo' about the idea of kinship that emerges from this kind of exploration. Instead, what the discussion reveals is a way of conceptualising reality that both reflects the complexity of that reality more fully than do our more familiar extractive metaphors, and also allows us to approach both other Humans and the more-than-Human world with a mindset that argues strongly against exploitation. Even in the atomised West, it is not acceptable to mistreat our kin. Take seriously the idea that a River can be an Ancestor, or a Dog a family member, and abuse of either one becomes infinitely less likely; find kinship in people and in beloved places, and build a connection that works against loneliness while making it easier to protect the people and places that are loved against the evils of community fragmentation and urban decay.

Or, as John Donne put it, in a different century and a different context: '*No man is an island, Entire of itself, Every man is a piece of the continent, A part of the main.*'

Homecoming

Everything is Connected to Everybody Else

Despite everyone's best efforts
(and their worst)

there is a deeper web
connecting everything that lives
and much that most would say does not.

It is still there despite
the way my mother took a broom and tried
to knock down all the cobwebs
that were lurking in the undercroft
(the dark entangling things)

and still despite
that moment years ago
when someone else – not you
stood where I stand now on this strand-line, listening

while millions of bubbles pinged
in weakening waves
and somewhere
in the distance, out of sight,
a man in a grey suit proclaimed the end of history.

The current here is depositional, leaving behind
a pebbled beach, a littoral strip
of red-brown fly-sand webbed between
the dropped rocks and the sea.
The line is not foot-friendly, being filled
with razor shells and sea-glass, but it's warm

and barefoot I walk gingerly upon

Homecoming

ground sandstone and grey granite
from along the coast
black-fly-ash-fly-black particles
enmeshed in water, bound by waves.

The present is a particle and wave.
I think. Like light.
Like space. Like everything.

Driving down today towards this coast
I passed the point where a few months ago I missed
my brother who had stopped here to assist
at the scene of a car crash. Travelling

on the same road, at the same time, quite by chance,
he and I happened both to be (almost)
in one identical location
when a stranger's car flipped over,
skidded on its side, sending up a cloud

of fly wave dust. He was on his way
to a recording session, amps stacked
in the far back of the van
and singer in the front seat. In her day job
she worked for the
Avon and Somerset Police. Within seconds

she'd secured the scene, called for support, alerted
Road Traffic Control, and summoned up
an ambulance. Strange chance,
that saves a stranger's life. Strange
chance that I should witness, driving
right on past it all and thinking
that could   /   that could never
have been me.

Homecoming

Today, while I was driving, stopped short at a red,
you were out, walking.
Somewhere, somewhere,
quietly just walking
onward through the limestone uplands
and fly-sand carved valleys of this seabed county.

Step by step, leaving all
your dusty imprints all along the holloways
and tunnelling between hogweeds bubbly with
snails and tangling spiderwebs.

Green light. I hit the gas, you stopped dead
at a stile. Somewhere in that great fly-webbed sea
the patterns shifted, old waves finally letting fall
cold sediment they'd gripped for centuries, casting
the black sand shoreward, building
up the strand-line, quietly.

Sea, car, dust, chance and you and me
and all of us entangled
still entangled, still

all travelling parallel
and here and here
on all these fly-dust-silver threads.

There is no there.
I think. There is

only the spiderweb,
the particle, the light.

Only the tide,
the sand, the wave.

Homecoming

Homecoming

List of Contributors:

Philip Shallcrass (Greywolf), is a writer, musician, artist and craftsman, who has been a Pagan since childhood and a Druid since 1974, founding the British Druid Order (BDO) a few years later. An instinctual animist, he has always thought of Iron Age Druids as the 'shamans' of much of Northwestern Europe, founding the BDO in part to promote this understanding within modern Druidry. Since 2006 much of his time, when not building roundhouses or making archaic musical instruments, has been devoted to researching, writing, editing and revising distance learning courses for the BDO. In 2023, he published a new, greatly expanded edition of his book, *Druidry: A Practical & Inspirational Guide*, which includes a rite parts of which featured in the closing ceremony of the London 2012 Paralympic Games. His *Greywolf's Lair* blog can be found at: **greywolf.druidry.co.uk**

Gordon MacLellan is a writer, poet and storyteller whose work explores the relationships between people, places, passion and wildlife. As Creeping Toad, he works with community groups to find ways of celebrating those relationships. Other writings include *Old Stones and Ancient Bones* (poems, direct from Gordon) and *Sacred Animals* (Green Magic Books, 2023) Find out more: **creepingtoad.blogspot.com / Social media: creeping toad**

Nancy N. Sidhu grew up on 4 ½ acres of wooded land in Connecticut, USA, and lives in Southern California with her husband. She worked as a teacher and broadcast journalist, and volunteered teaching dance (flamenco and hula), in climate change and solid waste planning, and as an Outdoor Ambassador.

Alison Elliott Married with three daughters I live in Paisley, the town which inspired me to write *This*. Completing a Masters in Creative Writing has built the confidence I lacked to focus on writing. I have contributed to school textbooks but *This* is my first creative writing narrative to be published.

Liv Torc is a poet, performer, participation expert, artist and project weaver, who plunders the vast caverns and dormant volcanoes of the human and planetary condition. Her books include *Show Me Life* (2015), *Banana Poems* (2021) and *The Human Emergency* (2021). As a poet Liv has been gigging for over 15 years and in 2022 performed at UN in Paris, appeared on BBCR4 Poetry Please and supported both Roger McGough and Hollie McNish in sell out shows. **livtorc.co.uk** to find out more.

Polly Paton Brown is an artist, writer and lover of the sacred, brings her experience as a trauma therapist working in the arts and eco and animal assisted therapy into all she does as a retreat facilitator. Polly's work will be featured in Lucy Pearce's upcoming book 'The Crow Moon'. She can be contacted via her website **www.pollypatonbrownartist.com**

Theresa Kelleher is a British Druid, poet and traditional storyteller. This year she received a Highly Commended Award in the National King Lear Prize 2023 and is the current Champion of the annual Leicester WORD Poetry Slam Competition 2023. Most of her work recognises the kinship and deep connection with all beings. She is currently working on her poetry collection *Mystical Tenderness.*

Susanne Mathies born in Hamburg, holds a PhD in economics and in philosophy. She has been living, writing and painting in Zurich for many years. Six of her German language crime novels have been published to date, most recently Mord mit Limmatblick, 2022, and Mord im Filmpodium, 2023, both at Gmeiner Verlag, Messkirch, Germany.

Liz Williams is a science fiction and fantasy writer living in Glastonbury, England, where she is co-director of a witchcraft supply business. She has been published by Bantam Spectra (US) and Tor Macmillan (UK), also Night Shade Press and appears regularly in Asimov's and other magazines. She has been involved with the Milford SF Writers' Workshop for over 25 years, and also teaches creative writing at a local college for Further Education.

Gareth N. Jones is an aspiring writer and photographer. He has travelled widely throughout Southeast Asia, with long stays in the Philippines and most recently in Japan. He is interested in how the environment shapes our identity, particularly in post-industrial landscapes such as the South Wales valleys where he is from.

S.V. Wolfland has published poetry and stories in the UK, USA, Canada and Australia, and *'Porlock the Warlock'*, a novel. S.V. has an MA in Creative Writing, is a professional storyteller who has performed at countless events, including regularly at Glastonbury Festival and who lives in the Pyrénées.

Carrie Osborne Working primarily in the visual arts as a picture framer, printmaker and illustrator, I have always had a deep love of language and creative writing, often combining poetry and prose with images in my arts practice. I often write about my own observations and responses to the natural world and the deep connectedness of all living things within in. I am particularly drawn to transitions in nature; seasons of light and dark, dawn and twilight, the cycles of life and death, storm-rise and ebbtide.

Helen Compton is a medical herbalist and lecturer in herbal medicine, undertaking a PhD while caring for her wonderful disabled partner and two neurodivergent sons in the wild green-grey of Yorkshire. Animist paganism has been her spiritual home for 30 years now, and she writes creatively where time allows.

Jack Wolf is a writer and academic whose first novel *The Tale of Raw Head and Bloody Bones* (Chatto and Windus / Vintage) was published to critical acclaim in 2013. Jack set up Aurochs Underground Press in 2022 in response to the urgent need to re-evaluate human relationships to one another and the Earth itself. Jack's second novel, *Mammoth and Crow*, was published by AUP in 2022, along with a poetry collection, *Dog Walking Weather.* To find out more visit: **aurochspress.co.uk**

Homecoming

Boann Lambert is a passionate artist whose work has a deeply feminine and intuitive approach which enables the creation of magical pieces of work in a range of mediums. Follow her on Instagram at **boannlambertartist**

Pinwydd Studio (Andressa Ferrari) I'm a Brazilian artist with a background in academic arts, but my love for old stories, ancient gods, and folk magic slowly shifted me towards pictorial storytelling and the Celtic lands. I currently live in Brittany, where I've been developing my practice towards narrative illustration and enjoying the wonder of giving life to the vivid characters, shapes and colours I see whenever words transport through charmed magic casements to the faery lands forlorn... Visit **pinwyddstudio.com** to see more of my work.

Note

Where contributors are based in the US, Canada or other countries where US spelling and punctuation rules are commonly used, these have been retained in accordance with the localist ethos of Animist practise.